Where Streams of
Living Water Flow

Where Streams of Living Water Flow

(The Adventure Of Walking With God)

PAUL LEWIS

emblembooks

www.emblembooks.co.uk

For Julie

CONTENTS

Acknowledgements 9

Foreword (by Freddy Hedley) 11

Into The Hills 15

Get Ready For Action 31

The Sword Of The Spirit 47

Dream Out Loud 65

One For The Road 79

Where Streams Of Living Water Flow 95

A Soundtrack To Your Life 107

The Adventure Of Walking With God 123

X Marks The Spot 137

So Beautiful 151

Last Orders 163

What About February? 175

Can You Cut It? 181

ACKNOWLEDGEMENTS

In a sense, this whole book belongs to God. Without Him, I would have nothing to write. All these stories, signs and the amazing guidance I have received on this adventure is all initiated by Jesus. Lord, how can I ever thank you enough?

Along the journey, I have travelled closely with a fellowship of true, honest companions that I wish to thank deeply for their ongoing support, encouragement and sense of fun and adventure. For Freddy - without you, I could never have published this book. A huge thank you for your insightful editing and wisdom. I am thrilled that walking inspired you to write a book as well!

For Steve - could there ever be a more loyal and trustworthy friend? Steve, you've journeyed with me across Britain and been with me through all the seasons of my soul - the highs and the lows. Cheers!

For my parents, Jane and Mervyn, who have generously lent me the resources that have enabled me to take off successfully. I owe you one!

For Nick - I guess we'll never forget that time at Land's End and Dartmoor when you came down to join me. You've been a real brother through it all. I am so pleased to see you adventure with the Lord in this way - long may it continue! Thanks also for the amazing photos you've taken for the book.

For Tom - thank you for those amazing walks in the Pennines and all our journeys across Snowdonia. You've put me up countless times in Leeds and have been a tremendous support for me in everything - thanks for the cricket analogies!

For Jane Bridger, thank you for your invaluable help in the proofreading you have done.

For Rob, my brother – what a sterling and imaginative effort you've made on the front cover. It's what everyone sees – thanks a million!

For my beautiful wife, Julie - I'll never forget when I first met you and I asked what you thought about chapter one. You cried - I'm glad it wasn't tears of boredom! You've been my soul mate and this book is for you. Now you need to write one yourself. No excuses, now!

To you, the reader - my prayer and hope is that you embark on the most amazing quest in your life and truly enjoy walking and adventuring with God. I would love to hear how God speaks to you and the journeys he has taken you on.

Go for it!

Paul Lewis

FOREWORD

It has been my privilege to be close friends with Paul for fifteen years. We have known each other for virtually the whole of each of our Christian lives and have shared many great memories, from sharing a house in Barnet in the late 1990s, to playing in bands together, to many hours spent in the wilderness.

In all that time, his passion for Jesus, and his expectation for hearing from God in dramatic ways, has always marked him out and been an inspiration. I have journeyed with him on several occasions where God has spoken prophetically to each of us, and in many cases I may well not have heard God's voice had it not been for the well-tuned eyes and ears of my good friend.

Over the years I have known many who are prophetic, many who are inspirational intercessors, and it has been wonderful to learn from them. I believe that Paul is one of these people – a humble man who has learned to tune his heart into God's voice, who has discovered for himself the adventure of walking with Him and is able to share that with others. A book exploring some of the insights he has gained over the years is long overdue!

What he has laid out in this book is part autobiography, part prayer journal, part theological exploration, and all inspirational. In it, Paul reveals some of the extraordinary ways that we can all hear prophetically from God and engage in the adventure He has set aside for us; he shares how this has worked in his own life; and he establishes a biblical foundation for his experience. At all times the language is accessible, digestible and full of encouragement.

Consequently, this is one of the best books on prophetic prayer I have read, and the only book on 'adventurous prayer' I have encountered! In short, this book can help make a dynamic prayer life more accessible, and that makes it worth its weight in gold.

I hope that what you find in these pages is the inspiration to try this adventurous prayer for yourself, that it leads to your own journal of dynamic prophetic experience, and that it helps to unlock a new depth to your personal relationship with God.

Freddy Hedley

Writer and Hub Director for Westminster Theological Centre in East Anglia

Look with your eyes and hear with your ears
and pay attention to everything I am
going to show you.

Ezekiel 40:4

CHAPTER ONE

Into The Hills

I want to run, I want to hide, I want to tear down the walls that hold me inside, I want to reach out and touch the flame — where the streets have no name.
Bono, U2

Picture this scene:

"Hang on, I'll be with you in a minute..."

"I'm nearly there – I'll call you right back!"

"Just give me five more minutes."

The last few weeks have been crazy. Deadlines, early morning starts and more and more pressure, working longer hours in a desperate attempt to keep the wolf from the door. In the midst of this you find yourself resorting to even more take-aways, because it's simply too much effort to cook anything remotely edible.

The stress of it all; voice mails on your mobile phone incessantly ringing you back asking for yet another favour; answer phone messages at home demanding your immediate attention and now, as if it couldn't be any worse, three big bills adorning your 'welcome' mat as you finally make it back from work. You're totally wiped out. So what now?

It's now time to play that ace of hearts you've had up your sleeve for weeks (you deserve it!). You simply can't take this any longer. That hotel you've booked on the coast in the national park with wild, unspoilt terrain on the doorstep – it's time for a much needed break. Perhaps the weather of your life could change?

It's that time when you desperately need to go into the hills, get that rucksack on your shoulder, hunger for solace and drink cool, refreshing water by a babbling brook and feel the sun on your face for the first time in weeks. It's time … not a moment to lose …

It's time to come 'home.'

After a long drive on the motorway, you eventually arrive in the pouring rain at the hotel – you've never been here before and your spirits rise as you see the manager come out to greet you. She asks how the journey's been and shows you your room – a first-floor bedroom overlooking the sea. Just what the doctor ordered.

There are pristine white sheets on the bed, coffee facilities at hand, a bedside radio, a shower unit…and the bar downstairs for a much-needed drink. Right now, though, as the rain lashes against the windowpane, it's time to hit the sack and you drift off …

Ever been there?

Well, that's exactly what happened to me one Friday night in May 2005. All that driving and effort to get here was infinitely worth it when I rose the following morning to find the sunlight bursting through the edges of the curtains. Wasting no time, I pulled them back to reveal an amazing view over the Bristol Channel.

The sea was dancing with light and seemed to gleam with the promise of a brand new day and offer a unique adventure on the horizon. And so, after a great night's sleep and a morning cup of coffee, I was wide-awake and desperate to get into the hills and lose myself in awe and wonder.

Already, the tiredness of the previous week had evaporated and London seemed like a planet I'd left behind light years ago. A full English breakfast greeted me downstairs and I'd brought my walk book with me. I simply prayed, "Lord, where would you like me to go today? Please show me the walk you've prepared for me since the creation of the world – please guide me to the one you have for me. Amen."

It's a simple prayer but I believe God has the very best for me and I want to be in the centre of His will – on the course He has set for me.

Invigorated and determined, I set off westwards from the hotel towards the Valley of Rocks – walking alongside a dramatic coastal path that literally hugged the cliff face, all the while savouring the stunning view of the sunlit, sweeping vista of the coastline of South Wales, captivated by the sheer energy of the waves crashing against the headland below and strong, bracing winds that threatened to blow me off course.

The next few moments were nothing short of absolutely fantastic – I was singing along to an album I'd not heard in a while, smiling, praising God and full of cheer. This cocktail of music, scenery, sun, freedom and worship elevated my spirit to new heights and I didn't want it to end.

Exploring the uncharted realms of my soul changes everything.

I think I must have smiled at everyone going by having gained a whole new perspective on everything. The stress of the last few weeks were washed away in moments and I began to thank God for who He is, the blessings He has poured out on me and for this wonderful opportunity. It was great talking to God like this. Not long after, I began to ask God to speak to me through signs and to my heart. I felt really alive.

This exhilarating coastal adventure was only just the beginning of something very special. Spending quality time enjoying intimacy with the creator of the universe amidst the backdrop of His beautiful creation is the nearest I can describe to being in heaven.

Within half an hour of finishing this walk by the sea, I headed for a remote region in the Exmoor National Park called 'The Chains.' This really was right into the wilderness: low stone walls for field boundaries, not a soul in sight, panoramic views across desolate moor lands, quiet farm lanes and the need for my compass to explore the terrain.

There and then I started to realise how much I'd longed for the chance to get into the hills, away from all the distractions and the manic pace of life and connect with My Heavenly Father – sharing everything with Him and enjoying His company.

This was the start of an epic adventure with Jesus and within a year, I was walking with God amidst the majestic beauty of the mountains in the Brecon Beacons (pictured below), enjoying the dynamic, rugged cliffs of the Cornish coast and being mesmerised by the breathtaking sunsets atop the fells in the Lake District.

The *real treasure* though, is hearing His voice and having my life changed as a result. Whenever I've revisited an area that I've explored, the one thing I remember above everything else is His life-giving streams of living water. Where these flow, there's nowhere else in the world I'd rather be.

At the very start of the film *Ben Hur* there is a subtle but nonetheless relevant scene when a local friend of Joseph visits him to enquire whether or not his table is finished.

Surprised when Joseph reveals that Jesus is neither home nor has completed the work in question, he remarks, "My table is not finished! Where is your son?"

"Walking in the hills," Joseph responds.

"He neglects his work, Joseph," comes the response back.

Then, Joseph turns round and states, "No. Once I approached him for forgetting his work, he said to me, 'I must be about my Father's business.'"

"Then why isn't he here, working?" demands his friend.

Joseph smiles, "He's working."

For those few moments, you see Jesus walking through the fields and into the hills beyond to spend quality time with His Father. I've never forgotten that scene since.

This isn't just a movie moment. The Bible tells us that Jesus got up very early each day to pray. He escaped the crowds and aimed straight for solitary mountainsides, lakes, forests and hills where he knew he wouldn't be disturbed. Take a look at these verses:

Very early in the morning, while it was *still dark*, Jesus got up, *left the house* and went off to a *solitary place*, where he prayed. Simon and his companions went to look for him, and when they found him, they exclaimed: "Everyone is looking for you!"
Mark 1:35-37

But Jesus often *withdrew* to *lonely* places and *prayed*.
Luke 5:16

One of those days Jesus went out to a *mountainside* to pray, and *spend the night* praying to God.
Luke 6:12

After this, Jesus and his disciples went out into the Judean *countryside*, where he spent some time with them …
John 3:22

Jesus, knowing that they intended to come and make him king by force, *withdrew again* to a *mountain* by himself.
John 6:15

Fascinating stuff, isn't it? Does any of this surprise you about your picture of Jesus? There's enough in these five verses alone to write an entire commentary but for now, let's enjoy plumbing the depths of some of these phrases in italics and perhaps we'll begin to paint a picture of Jesus' amazing 'diet of time' which, undoubtedly, formed the engine room of his entire mission and life.

Very early

I don't know about you but getting up at half past six in the morning on weekdays is a constant struggle for me - and always a losing battle with the snooze button on my alarm clock ("Just another five minutes …")! We've all been there. Is this *very early* in the morning, though? I doubt it. I reckon when Mark described Jesus' day it was more like half past four when the alarm went off.

If I got up at half past four in the morning in North London, where I live, what would it be like to go out and pray? Well, quiet for one thing! Virtually no traffic, no one about and no shops open. Quite a thought, isn't it? Crucially, though, there would be no distractions. Hours before the day has even begun for most people, Jesus is getting the finest quality time with His Father. If you've got a bible handy, just look at the incredible events, healings, conversations and astounding, confident teachings that follow – it's awesome!

However, for me, I don't think I can just roll out of bed when I like and be anywhere near as prepared as

He'd like me to be. Solid preparation is vital. Getting the 'heads up' on the day changes my whole perspective and feels like I'm putting on some 'heavenly' armour, making me fit and ready for any battle.

Mountainsides

Now this is curious. Why did he go up mountainsides? Having been walking, exploring and trekking for years, my guess is, it's probably because:

- Jesus' greatest desire was to spend quality time with His Father and get away from all kinds of distractions. This was of paramount importance. His whole life and ministry hung on quality times like these. It's quite an effort (if you've tried it) to scale a mountainside several hundred meters up and I would think most people wouldn't go up a mountain before setting off for work! No wonder, in one of the quotes above, we see his disciples try to search for him and say, "Everyone is looking for you!" I bet they were exhausted when they finally caught up with him!

- Mountainsides offer a unique perspective on life. If you've ever been in an aeroplane, it's fascinating to see the world you've just left behind: all the cars with their lights on, the street lights and everything that once seemed so big. They suddenly take on a new perspective. You begin to see things in a different way. It's as if the problems that have been dogging you and following you around all week are left on the ground and you (both physically and mentally) rise above them. You look down on where you were 'in the valley', what you purposely left behind and go onwards and upwards to explore, feeling enthusiastic at the promise of new territory up ahead, seeking to capture those 'summits' in your spirit that you know are really there, all the while, wearing your 'faith-tinted' glasses!

Lets' imagine you invited Jesus to stay at your house for a week. What would the experience be like? Would you frantically clear up to make the place spotless before he arrives, vacuuming like there's no tomorrow? Would you try and organise some inspiring visits to tourist 'cultural favourites' in your town? Would you spend hours in the kitchen, preparing your best recipes? Well, whatever happens, I'll bet it'll be seven days you'll never forget.

In fact, this very experience happened to two sisters called Mary and Martha but they both took totally opposite approaches. Martha did exactly what I've described above, whilst Mary did exactly what it says on the 'Maker's tin' – she desired nothing more than simply to hang out with Jesus. Rather than try and impress, she was just herself – no masks, no hiding behind busyness – she just wanted to 'be.'

Which camp would you be in? Here's the original account from Luke in the New Testament:

> As Jesus and his disciples were on their way,
> he came to a village where a woman named
> Martha opened her home to him. She had a sister
> called Mary who sat at the Lord's feet listening to
> what he said. But Martha was distracted by all
> the preparations that had to be made. She came to
> him and asked, "Lord, don't you care that my sister
> has left me to do all the work by myself? Tell her to
> help me!" "Martha, Martha, the Lord answered – you
> are worried and upset about many things, but
> only one thing is needed. Mary has chosen what is
> better, and it will not be taken away from her.
> **Luke 10: 38-42**

If you, like me, find yourself in 'Martha mode', just substitute your name for hers and read that paragraph again – it really hits the mark. At the heart of it all, it's all about relationship rather than ritual. Jesus' greatest desire here is to meet you where you are and talk with you personally.

Just think about that for a moment – wherever you are, whatever you're doing, Jesus wants to get alongside you and meet with you. The frantic vacuuming, the slaving over hot coals in the kitchen and the booking of tickets for the event in town have now hopefully been forgotten about – quality time in relationship is where it's at. That's where the gold is to be found.

Perhaps you're thinking (and have been, since page one) that your circumstances are totally different – that you can't just take off when you like and book into a Bed and Breakfast; or that you haven't got the time or energy to go climbing mountainsides; or that you struggle to get out of bed at half past eight, never mind half past four! Perhaps you don't like being alone.

The wonderful thing about the story of Mary and Martha is that you don't actually have to go anywhere. Just sitting at home talking to God is the best thing you can do. That intimacy is priceless. Mary wanted the refreshing water of God's spirit that Jesus offered her and so she sat with him - and it was for this reason she was commended.

As I write this very chapter, I find myself in Alnwick, Northumberland. This morning, I popped out for breakfast and the song that was playing in the café was none other than *Sit Down* by James. This was literally music to my ears, as the song perfectly sums up what I'm trying to say. Jesus is inviting us: "Sit down next to me."

So haven't I just contradicted myself? Not at all – the key in all of this is to find a place where *you* can genuinely pursue that level of intimacy with God, where you are not distracted, where you can allow yourself time to listen and drink from the fountain, where you can be yourself, where you can pray openly and honestly about anything on your mind, where you can just *be*, wherever the streams of living water flow for you.

The main reason I chose to write this book is because my own Christian life has been dramatically transformed by venturing out into the wild – finding that 'secret place' I was searching for all my life and simply being honest with God about everything.

Praying as I go in beautiful surroundings simply beats everything else. The first two verses in Psalm 121 sum this up perfectly:

I lift my eyes to the hills – where does my help come from? My help comes from the Lord, the Maker of heaven and earth.
Psalm 121:1-2

Amen!

It all started when I became a Christian at the age of twenty, whilst I was studying at Leicester University. The opening lines from U2's *Where The Streets Have No Name* brilliantly portray the sheer desperation of wanting to escape the suffocation of being fenced in, not able to pray out loud: "I want to run, I want to hide, I want to tear down the walls that hold me inside, I want to reach out and touch the flame – where the streets have no name."

This lyric perfectly paints the picture of embarking on an adventurous, exciting, faith-filled outward-bound quest with God, where there are no limits – the sense of freedom was simply exhilarating.

It all started when I began walking around Victoria Park in Leicester, praying that God would help me with my exams and that the right questions would come up – they did. But this was only the beginning, like a snowball gathering momentum rolling down a slope.

I began to seek out these 'mountainsides' and 'wildernesses' wherever I went. Working in Peru six months later, I escaped into the desert 'where the streets had no name' and had solace there. In the years after, when I worked as a teacher at schools in Barnet, I found local parks to disappear into, but *it's made all the difference.*

Whatever life throws at you, walking with God means you're never alone, as this song beautifully describes in the last two lines: "… and when I go there, I go there with you, it's all I can do …"

In June 2005, I was walking through Lydford Gorge in Dartmoor National Park, reflecting on how many times God had been so faithful in His mercy, grace, guidance and care – all the 'signs' he had shown me weren't just mere coincidences, but were actually guiding my life.

I simply couldn't keep it hidden under a bushel any longer. And so down the gorge I descended and then asked the question, "Lord, do you want me to write a book about all this? If so, what should I call it?" Immediately, I emerged at the base of a wonderful waterfall gushing from the top of the gorge and looked at it. The words, "Where streams of living water flow" entered my mind. It seemed to sum up everything I wanted to say perfectly.

So this is it. Walking with God is simply the best adventure anyone could ever have. Every time I've set out on a journey with God through the wilderness, I have to write it all down.

In the summer of 2007, I took myself off for three weeks to travel Britain – venturing out from the golden fields of Essex and windswept coastline of North Norfolk to the lonely but beautiful 'green desert' of Mid-Wales. From here, I drove south to explore the open moorlands of Exmoor on the North Devon coast, before finally making it down the end of the yellow brick road to St. Ives in Cornwall. This was a fascinating journey – all recorded in my 'adventure journal.'

I made an honest record of all my conversations with God during that time – dreams for the future, reflections on the past, thoughts of others and prayers for guidance and direction, giving thanks for how faithful and astonishing God has been in all areas of my life.

Looking back at this time, I am both encouraged and strengthened by seeing the incredible out-workings of those prophetic times of listening to God on those walks in the summer. Not just the leaps of faith that God urged me to take and the magnificent views to behold, but the essential insight into the forthcoming times of tremendous challenge, pressure and difficulty that I would face.

It's now time to get ourselves ready for action in the next chapter ...

CHAPTER TWO

Get Ready For Action

If I could, then I would, I'll go wherever you will go.
Way up high or down low, I'll go wherever you will go ...
run away with my heart ...

The Calling

Some basics

At first, it might seem strange having this as the second chapter but if you're up for more than just a 'one-off' adventure with God into the wilderness, this chapter will really help you prepare – both spiritually and physically.

The aim of this book isn't only to write about walking and have you properly equipped for that – there are plenty of helpful guidebooks out there which more than do justice to that. Instead, I'd like to highlight a few precious gems that could be worth their weight in gold on your forthcoming travels.

So, I'm going to take it for granted that you're probably wearing the right set of clothing for the adventure that lies ahead — whether it's a waterproof jacket you've got on, a rucksack strapped around your shoulders, your gran's best mittens to keep your hands from the cold or even a hat that makes you look like Indiana Jones!

Whatever your wardrobe, let's examine some essentials first...

Your mobile phone

You may think that I would be opposed to bringing a phone — that it somehow interrupts the adventure with God, but far from it! This is a really useful bit of kit for many reasons. Quite aside from the practical use of it being available in an emergency or for taking photos, having contact with the outside world, via text or phone calls, can be a powerful way for God to speak to you. Plus, it has one other very handy use ...

If you're serious about wanting to hear from God on your travels, then it's vital you write as you go, to create a journal or record that you will always have to look back on as a reminder of how God has spoken to you.

Of course, you don't have to use a mobile phone for this — you can simply use a pen and paper, or a receipt from your wallet or purse to jot things down, but I've found my mobile an excellent tool for noting down things as I go and saving them to memory, so they are added to your 'outbox.' You can edit these messages as you go, adding more detail in things you see, hear or sense God is saying to you.

Naturally, you don't have to do this but the beautiful moment might then be lost forever. You could get distracted and, before long, you've forgotten about it.

Later, when you get back home, write your quest up in a diary or journal of some kind and add the date. This discipline has many advantages. First, you get to 'download' your thoughts, prayers and messages you've heard from God. Secondly, one day, you'll look back and see how everything is fitting together – answered prayers, desires you had and where you were 'at.' Thirdly, you've now freed up some space, so your phone is ready to receive incoming texts!

In some cases, you might jot down so much, that your mobile phone's capacity is exceeded. What now? No pen? This happened to me once when I was in Cheddar Gorge down one of the caves. God was really speaking to me, not only through some of the names of the caverns, but through their stunning beauty and character.

While most people were using electronic headsets to hear the 'guide' leading them through the underground network of passages, I was busy texting! I'm sure some of them thought I was mad, as there's blatantly no reception in a cave! Forget about everyone else – if you sense God speaking to you profoundly, as was the case here, don't miss out – *write it down there and then!*

Ironically, I suddenly discovered to my annoyance that I had no space left on my phone (at the time I had quite an old phone with limited memory, but it still worked), so I wrote it all out and the minute I emerged out of the cave in the sunlight, I texted myself. I bet you're probably laughing – "How sad! He's got no friends, so he texts himself!" Far from it – this was a crucial piece of information that will impact me for the rest of my life. It might have cost me ten pence, but the rewards were priceless.

Walking boots

"These boots were made for walking," as the Nancy Sinatra song goes. Too right! An absolute must if you want to do any kind of cross-country walking, hiking and exploring.

Of course, there's nothing to stop you heading down the local park in your jeans, T-shirt and trainers, but if you really want something that's going to last a while and if you're keen to set out on journeys spanning several hours, then I'd recommend you get yourself a really good pair of boots that can cope with anything that nature throws at them.

I know it's tempting to go for a cheaper alternative, but you don't want your sole falling apart on Mount Snowdon or feeling the cold water creep in whilst picking your way across a muddy field in Devon.

At the end of 2001, I invested in an excellent pair of boots and I haven't looked back since. They've survived howling winds in Snowdonia, climbed icy, jagged peaks in the Lake District, crossed streams and rivers in the Brecon Beacons, protected me from frost bite in the deep snow of Quebec at temperatures of -6°C and trampled over dense undergrowth in Sherwood Forest.

It's not just about mastering the terrain, though. A great pair of walking boots gives you a wonderful boost of confidence and an enormous range of possible paths as you embark on your adventure of journeying with God and it means you don't have to think about whether they'll get you home or not.

There are plenty of verses in the Bible that make reference to walking, footwear and the Lord guiding our footsteps. For one, Paul cites the shoes as an essential part of our spiritual armour:

… and with your feet fitted with the readiness that comes from the gospel of peace.

Ephesians 6:15

Who knows whom you may encounter on your travels? If we are properly equipped with a desire to share God's love to those we come across we will go a long way. Just dipping into the Psalms and Proverbs, you'll discover that they're simply littered with gems of verses that will encourage you in your daily walk with God: "…

he set my feet upon a rock and made my footsteps firm" (Psalm 40:2b) and "In all your ways acknowledge him, and he will make your paths straight" (Proverbs 3:6). Wonderful promises, aren't they? God is *so* faithful.

In April 2007, after getting off the midnight train from Euston to Aviemore, I was chomping at the bit to hit the hills. It had been such a long winter of indoor activity, I was desperate to hike into the mountains with God and explore.

I can't really do justice to describing just what an exhilarating feeling it was, getting the rucksack on my back, strapping the boots on and setting off up the rocky, winding mountain path to the summits of the Cairngorms in Scotland. Blue sky all around, sun on my face and the sound of a mountain stream against a backdrop of a gentle breeze – this was such freedom!

Within minutes, my whole soul was lifted to new heights. The toll of busyness and the fallout of exhaustion were already evaporating in the sunlight of tranquillity. Invigorated, I pressed on into the mountains ahead, drew clear, cool water from a nearby mountain stream and ascended to the tops of the Cairngorms through deep snow.

It was just as well my boots were waterproof. On the return leg, the journey took an unexpected twist. I needed to be back at the car park to catch the last bus at ten past five and therefore, had to quicken my pace a bit (it was now half past three). The short stops on the way were well worth it, as the views were breathtaking, but I now needed to get my skates on.

"As long as I hold to a bearing of North-East, I should be fine," I thought.

A compass

Fortunately, I had one. But this story isn't finished yet: God had a few things to show me in this last hour and a half, which I'll never forget and I want to share them with you.

It really was vital that I stuck to my bearing of North-east, as the snow had completely covered the path, but in my haste to be back for the bus I made a small but significant error. I was so taken in by the stunning scenery in the distance and, keeping half an eye on the time, I inadvertently veered ever so slightly from my bearing. It was so subtle.

I didn't notice and continued for about twenty minutes, transfixed by the snow-capped mountains all around me. At ten-to-four, however, I was actually staring down the side of the wrong valley. Oh dear.

It's tempting to panic when you're on your own up a mountain you've never been on before, in the snow and feeling a bit lost. I prayed, "Lord, please help me." I took a few moments to calm down, take a few deep breaths and re-orientate myself to where I was supposed to be going. I also prayed that the Lord would show me the strategy and the timings, and that He would literally guide me.

I had to stick rigidly to my bearing this time but I felt the Lord encourage me to go slow and not rush. It's not a hundred metre dash home, more like a two-mile descent. It needed to be paced appropriately.

In actual fact, the snow was deeper than I thought but what made me even more concerned was the fact that I didn't know the type of terrain that lay beneath the snow. I assumed it was rocky outcrops but later discovered that what I was walking through was in actual fact a bog!

Friends of mine who have journeyed with me on my travels across Britain know that I've had a few mishaps like this! At the point I realised my situation, I had to be very careful and being on my own brought with it extra challenges. I looked to God for help. What I saw next was astonishing.

There was a set of footprints in the snow on a bearing of North-east! Just flick back to those verses in Psalms and Proverbs I mentioned before and you'll see what I mean. It was as if the Lord himself had walked ahead of me, guiding me safely home, showing me the way I couldn't see. This was excellent.

Had it been virgin snow, it is likely I would have stepped in the wrong places and fallen through to the bog beneath. But walking in these footprints assured me that someone had been before me and navigated the bog, and had left behind a safe route for me to follow.

In the end, I made it to the bus stop on the ski resort with five minutes to spare. But then someone kindly volunteered to give me a lift back to Aviemore. The photo below was from that day - all smiles before the bog!

This experience taught me several lessons – or rather, challenged me to ask several questions, which we can also ask of one another: Is the compass in our heart pointing to God? Are we sticking to his bearing or are we tempted to veer off the path and get distracted with other things, no matter how appealing they might be? Do we ask the Lord to guide us regularly and more to the point, do we trust Him?

I learnt more about God's faithfulness, guidance and care for me up that mountain than I did in a thousand days at my desk.

A compass is such a vital piece of equipment that takes up virtually no space, takes a moment to learn to use and costs no more than ten quid. But it could save your life. It's been invaluable to me on my travels, determining the right paths through forests, orientating myself with the map and, of course, trekking through snow.

However, all such adventures also require energy. A packet of ready salted crisps might be tasty, but won't sustain you on treks like these...

Essential provisions

Sometimes, I've been so eager to set off into the wilderness exploring, that I have forgotten to pack anything to eat or drink. So I need to remind myself that they are essential!

Of course, it's not my place to suggest a certain diet for you. Neither is it necessary to pack an entire wicker picnic hamper full of French bread, a selection of cheeses, a chilled drink and bunches of fresh grapes. Although far be it from me to stop you! All I'm saying is, depending on the length and difficulty of your walk, take appropriate sustenance with you. It's always a good idea to have some nourishment for the journey ahead.

A round of sandwiches with some fruit, crisps and a muesli/chocolate bar should suffice, together with an all-important bottle of water. Never underestimate the value of a good flask of cool, refreshing water. In the summer months especially, you can lose a lot of moisture through sweat. In the words of Ray Mears, "if you sweat buckets, then you need to drink buckets."[1]

I've occasionally set off without eating anything beforehand and consequently, have found myself thinking of food for most of the way, undermining the reason for setting out in the first place! Of course, you might have planned your walk strategically to incorporate a café en route or at the end, as a reward for your efforts. In this case, you have a justifiable reason in minimising which of the provisions above you take.

If you're planning a highland quest, there are often plenty of upland streams that you can fill up from, but be careful with these – check where the source is likely to be first. Establish if the water is clear; if it's neither standing water nor relatively slow moving, you're doing well. If it's not at a low altitude and doesn't have a flock of sheep immediately above it, you can start drinking!

Just as we need water to sustain us and refresh us, we also need the "streams of living water" that Jesus himself wants us to drink from, "in which we will never thirst and will be a spring of water welling up inside us to eternal life" (John 5).

If we choose to go without *this* water from the Lord, we'll miss out in a big way. More on this as we venture forth.

---

[1] Ray Mears, *Extreme Survival* (series 1), episode one: Rainforest.

A map

Where would you be without one? Lost, I presume! To really get the most out of adventuring with God in places you haven't seen before, I suggest buying a map and/or guidebook for a particular area.

It could be a national park, area of outstanding natural beauty or a large-scale map of your local area. Initially, this will test your O-level or GSCE geography skills, which can be quite fun, but as you become accustomed to the great outdoors, you'll want to walk further, explore more and break further and further out of your comfort zone.

What I love most about doing a walk in an 'unexplored' area is the sheer anticipation of looking forward to the God of the entire universe wanting to communicate with me on a personal level. Nothing beats this.

Lift everything to Him. Ask Him to show you which walk He wants you to do, and when and where. Invite Jesus to walk with you and to speak to you through anything – signs, creation, animals, people, birds, the weather, rivers, songs on your personal stereo (if you're using one), words on the map, features, monuments, valleys, buildings, pubs, street names, registration plates, town names, churches, schools, road markings, text messages ... the list goes on.

God knows the best way to communicate with you – just ask! This is the adventure I'm writing about and it keeps me wanting more of Him every time I set out.

However, don't bite off more than you can chew on your first outing. Don't attempt to climb Ben Nevis if all you've done is a walk around the cheese counter at Tesco's last night! Start with small, local outings around the park or down your street – anywhere where you can get clear of distractions (see the chapter nine for some ideas).

Spend a few moments in prayer before you set out – ask God to speak to you personally through the walk you're about to have. Is there a situation that's really on your mind or something that's bugging you? Be honest – ask God for advice. He loves to hear from you – just pick up the 'phone!'

Last but not least, pace yourself. Most walk books I use have checkpoints (letters or numbers) strategically positioned to split up the journey into sections. This is really helpful, as you can plan each part of your adventure in, say, half-hour chunks, making it much easier and less pressured to reach the next checkpoint, helping you factor in times of rest and breaks for much needed refreshments.

Having a map releases you into these adventures with God. And of course, God gives us all a map to help us find our way through life with Him – but we will talk more about this in the next chapter.

A camera

Whether it's digital, on your mobile or a disposable one you bought at the petrol station last weekend, it's worth bringing a camera. Not just for scenic appreciation or doing poses for album covers on the Cornish coast, but to record your adventures.

Years later, when you look back at your pictures (especially the stranger ones!), it's a wonderful reminder of how God spoke to you back then. These are encouraging times and it's great to make your own unique album of wilderness adventures.

In chapter one I told you how I felt God was speaking to me about writing this book, how I asked what it should be called and I turned a corner to see an incredible waterfall and the words, "Where streams of living water flow" came straight to me. Well, praise God that I had taken my camera with me, so the moment could be captured and returned to.

When approaching a walk, try not to just look at it as a means from getting from A to B. God is just as interested in your journey as He is with your destination. Take time to savour every moment along the way. It could be pausing for a moment to capture an amazing picture of a glorious view across the mountains or to be captivated by a beautiful sunset.

Perhaps take time out to enjoy exploring a ruined castle or, as Otis Redding put it, to "sit on the dock of the bay," chill out to a relaxing piece of music or simply rest by the lakeshore and enjoy the sun on your face while reading a book.

I remember being in the Lake District in 2001 and doing just that: sitting by Tarn Hows, reading the Bible before setting off on the long walk I had prepared for that day. I sat there for more than two hours, being illuminated by God's Word and astounded by the sheer beauty that surrounded me. In the end, I abandoned the walk and simply allowed myself to rest in His presence and read a most fascinating book.

It is to these pages we now turn ...

CHAPTER THREE

The Sword Of The Spirit

In the closing weeks of 2006, I set out on an adventure through the mist and rain in the heart of England on what could only be described as a 'mysterious' afternoon. The fog became so thick, I could barely make anything out.

To my surprise, I came across a wonderful shop in a town filled with antique swords, guns, shields and armour. It was a real goldmine of adventurous treasures. I was drawn at once to the wide selection of impressive, gleaming swords in the window and I just couldn't resist examining these artefacts more closely. Most of them were hundreds of pounds and far beyond my means, but one struck me straight away. It was four feet long and looked the business. What's more, this one was affordable and, when I looked closely, it included the inscription, 'Ancient Warrior.'

I simply had to buy it. Both as a collector's piece and also because it felt like this was God's symbolic present to me. Not only was it wonderfully affirming but also, this served as a real challenge to take up the Sword of the

Spirit and put it to effective use in the spiritual battles I will face in this life.

The Sword of the Spirit is one of the vital pieces of spiritual armour that Paul describes in his New Testament letter to the Ephesians (read Ephesians 6:10-20). This is a brilliant picture of a Christian's 'heavenly' protection, identity and battle-gear intended for spiritual warfare and was inspired by looking closely at a Roman soldier's uniform: equipped with the breastplate of righteousness in place, the belt of truth buckled around the waist, protected by the helmet of salvation and feet fitted with the readiness that comes from the gospel of peace and protected by the shield of faith. The last (but not least) piece is an offensive weapon – the sword of the Spirit, which is the Word of God:

> Put on the full armour of God so that you can take your stand against the devil's schemes. For our struggle is not against flesh and blood, but against the rulers, against the authorities, against the powers of this dark world and against the spiritual forces of evil in the heavenly realms.
>
> **Ephesians 6:11-12**

I recall, as a boy of fifteen, playing a challenging computer adventure game with my brother Rob. It was set in a 'medieval' type world with knights, castles, caves, damsels in distress and finally a warrior, who sets out on a perilous quest to destroy the evil that threatens the land and stops at nothing to restore peace to the kingdom he loves.

It's a familiar story, but nonetheless captivating and engaging – it took us months to complete (including many late nights), but was definitely worth the effort. What I remember most about the story was the fact that we could upgrade the armour. The finest swords, shields and armour all had to be *discovered* (and were often in the trickiest places), but there was one special weapon that was by far the most difficult to find: the silver sword.

This was the most sought-after weapon of all throughout the kingdom, and when we finally acquired it, the result was simply devastating - inflicting enormous amounts of damage with one slash to the evil creatures that threatened to conquer the land and wipe out the lives of others.

This sword really was magnificent. It won us the game. We *never* put it down and certainly *never* dreamed of trading it in for anything else.

The Sword of the Spirit that Paul refers to is, in fact, the Bible. Let me ask you – do you see the Bible as a sword – an offensive weapon to wield against evil? A scimitar of truth that deals a hammer blow to demonic forces and sets the captives free? Just how often, how skilfully and how enthusiastically do any of us wield this powerful weapon?

Now, this is a challenge – and one where I am continually put to the test. It requires discipline, commitment, prayer and regular, systematic use if we are to make the very best of God's Word. This sword, if used to its full potential, is life-giving to us and will utterly devastate the enemy's strongholds.

Not only does God's Word inspire, encourage, strengthen and fill us with hope, it offers us incomparable wisdom for every situation we find ourselves in. It also cuts through lies, throws light on people's motives, exposes evil strongholds and provides us with unparalleled insight to demolish them, making visible a path for us in life.

Furthermore, the pearls of wisdom contained within its pages could, if applied, offer a timely word of encouragement to a friend of yours who desperately needs it, or even a much bigger dose of love to set someone free. And that's not all – beyond all of these is the truth that these are God's very words to us and yes, the God of the universe, the creator of life itself, wants to communicate with you. These are His words to us throughout history to give us life.

So, the question remains – will you open the book? Or, like Excalibur stuck in the rock for centuries, does the Bible you have still reside on a shelf somewhere in your attic, just waiting to be plucked out by a hero, polished up and bravely held aloft victoriously to go into battle and see people set free? The choice lies with you.

Let's imagine this scenario:

It is many hundreds of years ago. There you are, toiling away in the fields as a farm labourer, day in, day out, under a hot sun. It's been peacetime for as long as you can remember – once or twice, someone in your village offered you the chance to hold and practice using a broadsword. You declined the offer, explaining that in all the years you've lived at home, there's never been a raid, a war – not even a rumour of one. In your local tavern, you even went so far as to mock the very idea of anyone with any sense bothering to attack your village.

"There's nothing worth taking," you said.

Then, suddenly one afternoon, literally from out of nowhere, a distant clunking of metal, the thudding of a thousand hooves and a dust cloud rising on the horizon makes your blood run cold and for a moment you freeze. "Nothing worth taking..." You wished you'd never been so silly.

Nobody in the village knows what is happening, until you bolt down the lane, swinging a rake in your right hand and screaming at the top of your voice that an army is coming. Suddenly, there is a furious panic – people diving for cover, confusion all around, crying babies and others shouting orders.

No-one really knows what is going on – are we being attacked? The noise behind you becomes deafening and you scramble for the barn to protect a handful of children that you've seen gather there in distress, hiding behind the haystacks and barrels. To your left, on the ground, you see that very same broadsword you had previously declined. This is no rake. You wish you'd practiced with it when you were given the chance.

Without hesitation, you pick up the two-handed blade (which weighs a ton) and stand resolutely, with the children behind your back, and desperately try to convince yourself that you can wield this weapon like a gladiator fighting for freedom in the Colosseum.

There is a lot of noise outside and you can hear the commander giving the order for his soldiers to dismount and break open the barn door. At this moment, your heart nearly bursts through your chest and you fear the worst. Within seconds, the barn door is smashed open and about twenty soldiers suddenly rush into view.

Everyone looks straight at you. The command comes from the captain for you to drop your sword but you're brave enough to ask, "Why?" The truth is, as you've never seen any soldiers or armies before, you know nothing of the markings on banners, flags and coats of arms. You are presuming that this is the enemy.

The reply comes, "We have received word that our borders are about to be attacked in the next few days. We're gathering as many weapons, as much armour and as many volunteers as we can to help defend our land in this emergency. Will you fight?"

So, what would you do, then?

I'll leave the story there for you to fill in the blanks of what happens next, but this does raise crucial points. You needed the sword to defend yourself and the lives of others. A rake is pitifully inadequate. You needed practice with the sword. What if it was a raiding party from the enemy? They needed that sword for battle. They needed you.

Just substitute the word 'sword' for the phrase 'Sword of the Spirit' (Ephesians 6) and the word 'enemy' for 'Satan.' Now read the story again. Do you see just how absolutely crucial the Bible is to us? Actually, I hope you put this book down right now and grab the real thing. It is such a phenomenal gift of God – one that can speak right into your life at this very moment and we need to get to grips with it.

At this point, objections and questions often begin to rise for many. Questions like:

- "OK, I have a bible but I haven't read it for years."
- "Where do I start? Genesis or Revelation?"
- "How do I read it? All in one go?"
- "What translation is best?"

They can feel like stumbling blocks – reasons to be daunted by God's Word – but they also reveal a heart to know that Word better, to take the Sword of the Spirit seriously, and tackling these questions head on will always open up Scripture more. So, if you're asking any of these questions, that's great! The first few times may well seem like you're swishing about in thin air and thrusting randomly in any direction, but don't worry!

An excellent strategy is to pray just before grabbing the hilt. Ask God to speak to you through His Word and trust that He will.

What I find best is to buy a booklet of Bible-reading notes (there are loads available). These give your reading a structure and order, as well as helping with understanding or hearing what God is saying. In my experience, its best to attempt this earlier in the day, as it sets you up perfectly and, rather like a piece of succulent fillet steak, chew on it as the day unfolds - let it get into your system.

Others, though, may read at different times, depending on what suits them best. The key is to find a rhythm that works for you. It should:

- Be a rhythm you can keep with little discipline;
- Benefit your rhythm of life between work and rest;
- Still take priority over other things.

The last point to mention is all about setting a portion of your life aside to hear from God. Putting other 'important' areas of life down for a moment is a clear sign that you mean it.

Often, as you read, you may not be able to see the relevance straight away but I have found that situations have presented themselves later on in the day, where the wisdom gleaned from reading the Word has given me a massive advantage in tackling the dilemma before me and has also resulted in blessing others through it. And, even more importantly, giving God the glory. It really is an amazing adventure – the Creator of the Universe speaking to you and me personally and right into the very heart of the current situations that we face.

No-one likes to live their life on their own - just to know that God Himself is with you makes all the difference.

I remember vividly the first time I *really* read the Bible. It was 1994. I'd just become a Christian and it felt the whole world had suddenly changed within me. I began to see things in a very different light and it was tremendously exciting. Yes, I'd heard stories of Noah's Ark, David and Goliath, Moses and the Ten Commandments when I was a child, but that was about it.

I'd heard these stories, but never actually read them for myself. The sheer joy in discovering God's Word for the first time was unforgettable – I soon found myself on an Indiana Jones-type quest exploring the Bible in depth. Investigating the historicity, excavating the authenticity and searching for answers I'd always sought to the questions I had.

I could hardly believe what I'd missed out on all these years! I soon made up for it though. One evening I was up until nearly quarter to two in the morning, utterly absorbed in reading Acts of the Apostles right to the end. But, as you'll discover shortly, this is no mere 'story book.'

As we will see throughout this book, God speaks to us in a huge variety of ways. And when he does so, it always the right words at the right time. There have been countless times when I have been left dumbfounded by the sheer precision, the supernatural timing of God's words.

Let me give you an example from when I was trusting God for my first full-time job. I was desperate to do it *His* way in *His* time. I must have applied to a good handful of secondary schools towards the end of my probation year as a teacher. I made it to the interview process a number of times, but never seemed to get the green light.

By then, just about all of my colleagues at University had got jobs lined up for September, but not me. I kept praying and trusting. Throughout all this, I was reading the Word regularly. I was following the account of Joshua leading the Israelites into the Promised Land. Not only did the promises ("I am with you, I will never leave you") regularly feature in reminding me of God's provision and love, but the whole theme of new beginnings and a new start came into a sharp focus. I experienced a growing feeling throughout, that God was leading me into the promise of a fantastic new job.

At one point, things seemed to be getting desperate. It had been a while since any job opportunity had arisen and all the advertisements in the *Times Educational Supplement* seemed to have dried up. I decided to go and pay a visit to the local cricket nets (at my old school) to play a few shots.

Almost immediately on arriving, before I had chance to get started, the heavens opened and across the playing field strolled my former PE teacher. He asked what I was up to and I mentioned (apart from wanting to bat) that I was actually in the process of looking for a job teaching geography. He replied that only the day before, one of the current members of staff teaching geography had announced that he was to leave at the end of the academic year. I was stunned. Within days, I applied to the school for the post and I was the only one at the interview. I got the job and began an enjoyable and fulfilling job, which lasted for seven years.

Just think for a minute about the great commission Jesus gave us (Matthew 28:16-20). The great CO-mission. We're not supposed to be on our own, as lone rangers. Life is about adventuring with the Lord through everything you encounter, journeying with Him through the roads of your soul, negotiating the 'traffic' that comes your way.

Life is a map waiting to be explored and the journey is just as important as the destination. Who knows the adventure God has for you today? Do you want Him involved in that experience, to lead you, to help you? At the end of the day, the most important thing ever is our relationship with God. That's why we're made. We were made in God's image to connect with Him and to have an amazing relationship with Him.

After a crazy September, I was desperate for a much-needed rest, so I set off for Sheringham on the North Norfolk coast in search of solace, relaxation and some serious battery recharging! The word of the day for the Saturday was none other than Psalm 23 – right on cue! Just what the doctor ordered. If you're not familiar with this psalm, take a quick look at it now and you'll see what I mean.

That pause, that break, did me the world of good … but there was more. The following morning came the story of Mary and Martha (Luke 10:38-42). We have already looked at this in chapter one so you will probably understand its significance! God didn't want me to miss out on what really mattered – quality time with the King. It was so encouraging and affirming that God's priority for me that weekend was to get away from distractions, to slow down, chill and hang out with Him. Nothing else mattered.

Be prepared, though. I believe God wants the very best for us and like gold being refined in a furnace of fire, we need to expect to be challenged in many areas of our lives – this process burns off the impurities of indifference, revealing the original 'heart', the jewel that lies deep within us.

The Bible is also the 'spirit level' we need to weigh and measure everything we see, hear and experience in life. This is why this chapter features so early on in the book, as the Bible provides a perfect platform for listening to and hearing from God.

Imagine for a moment that you are a construction worker on a building site, helping to lay the foundations of a house for a family – *your* family. Naturally, you'd want to get it absolutely right. If the foundations are not right, nothing else will be. Not to use a spirit-level would be unthinkable – just think what would happen if you got it a few degrees out. Can you imagine having a bath?!

One of the vital points I wish to underline in this book that underpins everything else, is that we should always weigh carefully any signs we see, experiences we have or impressions that form in our minds, with the authority of Scripture. Read these words from 2 Timothy:

All Scripture is God-breathed and is useful for
teaching, rebuking, correcting and training
in righteousness, so that the man of God may be
thoroughly equipped for every good work.

2 Timothy 3:16-17

If what we hear doesn't fall in line with Scripture, then it's off beam and isn't from God. Let the Sword of the Spirit be your spirit level and stay within the limits; just two degrees out in a crucial decision or move could be the difference between a success and a failure.

The consequences for both could be far-reaching. The Bible itself encourages us to "test and approve what God's will is – his good, pleasing and perfect will." (Romans 12:2)

God will never tell us to do anything that is at variance with Scripture. If you are unsure, then share your thoughts and impressions with a trusted friend whom you can be accountable to. After all, there is an encouraging passage in the Bible that states, "A cord of three strands is not quickly broken." (Ecclesiastes 4:12)

Furthermore, we should remember that we never fight alone and that we have a 'commanding officer' who loves us and knows what is best for us. This, then, raises the question of ...

Guidance

I want to ask you in all seriousness, what first comes to mind when you hear or read this word? Be honest – is it a 'red marker pen', which threatens to fence in your freedom? Or a set of stabilisers for your life that seem patronising? Or is it actually a welcome spot of advice that you couldn't really do without? The Bible describes itself as "a lamp to my feet and a light for my path" (Psalm 119:105).

As a man (and also as a geography teacher), I hate getting lost! One of the worst things anyone can say to me is, "Are you lost?" It's pride, unashamedly of course, as I don't want to admit to anyone that I couldn't follow a simple map.

One sunny August day in 2006 in South Wales, a group of nine of us set out on a challenging four-hour trek through the forests, hills and valleys of the Brecon Beacons. I had the map and the compass and led the expedition. About three-quarters of the way through, we reached a small farm, a very old church and paused at a junction of paths. As I stopped to look at the map to plot the way ahead, my friend Jenny asked me, "Paul, are you lost?"

My reaction wasn't calm, to say the least! I was simply temporarily unaware of my precise co-ordinates! It does, however, raise a good question.

How many of us stop to ask for directions? It needn't be an embarrassing experience or one of dented pride, but actually a humble approach to life and, moreover, a brilliant attitude when following God's plans and desires for our lives, remembering always that He wants the best for us.

When I was a child, I loved building things with Lego. Castles, spaceships, train stations, buses, aeroplanes. Within hours, entire lunar landscapes or half-finished towns covered the living room floor. I loved the creativity that it offered. I could simply build anything I wanted and spent every waking hour thinking up hugely ambitious scenes and littering the carpet with hundreds of coloured bricks, much to the annoyance of everyone else!

What I couldn't do without, though, was the instruction manual that came with each set. Whenever I built a model for the first time it was the first thing I reached for. I was fascinated to see how the 'master builder' intended it to be and how it all came together. Have you ever tried building a big Lego spaceship without the instructions?

I never saw the instructions as stifling my freedom, but rather having a *journey* to experience and when I first looked at all the pieces, I wondered what role each part would eventually play in producing the finished model. Some pieces would never be seen by anyone looking at the finished product but without them in place it would soon fall to bits!

In the same way, you could describe the Bible as God's instruction manual for our lives. The Master Builder has a great plan for our lives – do we want to follow His instructions or disregard them?

A part of the army

The Bible is our instruction manual – or map – and it is also our greatest weapon in spiritual battles. But just before you pick up your sword and wield it, let's remind ourselves that we're not alone in this — it's not about trying to be Conan the Barbarian.

We must put to use the rest of our spiritual armour, which we urgently need to equip ourselves with, so we can effectively hear from and be used powerfully by Jesus. Armed with our swords, and standing side by side, we become like a unified Roman battalion of soldiers — shields locked together, armed to the teeth and ready for, "whatever comes out of those gates," as in the scene from *Gladiator* when a group of slaves were faced with the seemingly overwhelming odds as chariot after chariot streamed towards them in the Colosseum.

How did they survive? They not only used their weapons and armour extremely well, they stuck together as a team and presented a unified front, against which the enemy simply had no answer and consequently they won a remarkable victory, against all the odds.

This is a marvellous picture of the church. If you are not currently a member of a church, or if you desire to be an essential part of a tight-knit family of believers who stand together, believing in God's powerful Word, praying for you and others and sharing their lives with each other, why not join one?

The support, strength, unity, joy and togetherness you will experience could well change your life and enable you to face any odds, no matter how overwhelming they appear to be.

As we close this chapter, ask yourself this question: What is God's plan and purpose for you? If you could do anything and live out your dreams, what would you do? God has a plan for you that is beyond your wildest dreams.

Do you dare trust Him?

CHAPTER FOUR

Dream Out Loud

Think of a movie you saw recently that you connected with – that you really engaged with at a deep level, that left you wishing it was you right there in the spotlight – a movie which triggers that rising feeling within you that makes you think, for just a moment, that *you* can change the world or transform someone's day by the words you say or the heroic action you perform to rescue them from a 'pit' they're in and set them free.

This time, however, don't let the memory of that moment fade - choose to stay with it. If you've begun to use the Sword of the Spirit, you will have discovered just how much God loves you and the lengths He goes to fight for you. I hope you're starting to realise who you are – the diamond He had in mind before you were even born. Yes. Don't let it fade away – run with it and fly with it. Dare to dream out loud.

There is a poignant scene in the final film of the *Lord of the Rings* trilogy, *The Return of the King*, when Elrond implores Aragorn on the eve of battle to, "Put aside the ranger; become who you were born to be." He saw the leader in this man. What's more, Elrond recognised who Aragorn really was.

Know the truth that God has set you apart for a unique role in His plan – a central character in the script. It is your licence to dream out loud. Don't let anyone steal it from you. Now tell me, *just what is it that you really want to do?*

Imagine there are no barriers to your finance, no robbers of your time and no roadblocks to your destiny. Let it surface and dare to tell yourself about the dream you have. Even better, go and tell someone else! Then, talk to your Heavenly Father about all you want to do, what you want the story of your life to be.

Now go for the impossible. Get beyond your circumstances, what society expects of you, leave rationality behind and savour the freedom of totally going for it – the things you'd never have dreamt of seeing or doing. Imagine the answer to the question, "Why am I here?"

Let's do away with small planning, the 'low hills' around the backyard and go flat-out for the full-on adventure He has for you in the very essence of who you are. Will you pursue this – the greatest adventure God has for you, or will you slip out of the movie halfway through and quietly file your dream in a folder marked 'Don't be silly?' It's a challenge, but one that's definitely worth it.

One of the phenomenal things about God is that He is the God of the impossible. So, you don't need to stress out about whether it's financially viable or not, or worry if it's politically correct. Was Moses denied access across the Red Sea? Was Abraham denied a son at a grand old age? No. Look closely at Jesus' invitation to 'dream out loud':

Ask and you will receive; seek and you will find; knock and the door will be opened to you. For anyone who asks, receives; he who seeks finds; and anyone who knocks, the door will be opened.

Matthew 7:7-8

That's *you* he's encouraging. He loves you. He wants the best for you.

In August 2008, I was glued to the television set and wired to my radio in the early hours of the morning, watching and listening to some of the incredibly moving and inspirational scenes of the Olympic Games in Beijing. Witnessing the overjoyed faces of ecstatic athletes achieving the dreams they'd dared to believe – not just competing in the Games, but performing to an audience of billions, giving it their absolute all in the event of their lives.

Tears of emotion, shouts of joy and celebrations of victory are what it's all about. These people dreamt out loud at high volume. They didn't settle for anything else and certainly didn't settle for anything less.

Did you catch any of it? One interview on the radio said it all. Alan Campbell, rowing for Great Britain in the single skulls event, gave everything he had in the final – and this incredible effort was made even more special by the fact that this was on the back of months of injury. His mother, asked afterwards for her thoughts on her son's performance said, "Those who do not dream do not live." This was so inspiring.

The time for whispering on the line may have to go. Be bold. Shout it out! If you can get some time alone with God in the car, or you're out walking the dog, or praying out loud in the bath, or in the office when no one's around, that's a great start.

Tapping into God's eternal destiny and the plans he has for you are simply awesome – they could also be eternally significant for others. Imagine their lives changing. Just take a look at these words from Jeremiah:

> For I know the plans I have for you," declares
> the Lord, "plans to prosper you and not to
> harm you, plans to give you a hope and a future.
> Then you will call upon me and come and pray to me,
> and I will listen to you. You will seek me and find me
> when you seek me with all your heart.
>
> **Jeremiah 29:11-13**

Amazing promises, aren't they? Go on, apply these words to yourself. This should banish any lurking shadows of fear, blow away any cobwebs of anxiety and shatter any illusions of low self-esteem.

If you were the boss of a firm offering a job to someone, let me ask you this: would you prefer a determined applicant or a casual enquirer? Yes, it may well come to some serious praying: crying out loud, being broken in two, cut to the heart and collapsing to the floor, pleading and screaming out to God with tears streaming down your face, but at least you're serious about it and you do not want to settle for mediocrity – you want your prayer answered!

Rest assured – God is listening to what you're saying and is *fighting for you.* Think back to the movies you thought of at the beginning of the chapter. I bet the hero's journey wasn't easy – and neither was that of Joseph's, Noah's, Elijah's or Paul's in the Bible; not to mention that of Jesus'.

It's not going to be easy, because we're in a spiritual battle. In 2006, I was in the centre of a real storm in life, where incessant waves from all manner of physical, financial, emotional and spiritual directions pounded against my ship with devastating force. This lethal combination nearly finished me off. It was time to ask the impossible, dream out loud and plead for divine intervention. I needed rescuing.

I had been in my second teaching post, at St Mary's School for a few years but had sensed that it was time to leave, to take a risk to pursue ministry work in the community – something I'd always wanted to do.

The area of community work I was particularly excited about starting was that of leading a Street Pastors team in Barnet.

Practically speaking, however, setting out as a self-supported community worker was a big risk. I had little financial support and I would be leaving a teaching post that was my only source of financial stability and security. But I needed 'time out' to launch this project properly and give it everything I had. "What do I do, then, Lord?" I prayed.

About a week later, I set off for a few days' exploring in Devon. Lydford Gorge just happened to be en route to where I was heading. Remember this one? Yep, I couldn't possibly resist. I decided to pray about my future.

Immediately after the spectacular reminder of *that* waterfall, a little boy ran ahead of me on the winding path next to the stream and his mum shouted out "Wait!" Two minutes later, another boy appeared with the word GAP on his sweater. Wow. Does this mean I need to take a 'gap' or some time off, before ploughing into another job straight away?

The thought of taking a break from it all was music to my ears. I felt that not only does God want to bless me and reward me with a kind of 'sabbatical,' after ten years of teaching but He wants me to trust Him in a way that I have never done before. So, for the remainder of the walk, I pondered on this possibility and the timescale that God may have in mind.

As I drove on to the Seawood Hotel on the north coast, it was developing into a beautiful evening. I couldn't help but notice the countless signs on the roads, saying *Slow* and *Slow Down* and I sensed the Lord wanted to give me this 'gap' to enable me to focus wholeheartedly on developing the community, church and Street Pastors work.

I still had energy in the tank for another adventure and I wanted to pursue God more on this same issue. I wanted to strike while the iron was hot. The cliff-top scenery around the foreland was stunning. There was blue sky and the sun illuminated everything around me. It was to become a walk I would never forget.

As the sun was setting, I felt the still, small voice of God asking me if I really did trust Him and His provision enough to make this 'leap of faith.' I knew this involved completely giving up my job and relying on him. This was very challenging, as I had never done this before, but I sensed His love and warm embrace and I knew deep down that this was an opportunity not to miss – and one which would strengthen my and others' faith tremendously. I decided there and then to let go and trust God completely.

Towards the beginning of September (when the money had dried up from teaching), I was having a bath one evening and I prayed for some money to help me pay for the rent and my living expenses. I asked the Lord for £500. The next day, a cheque arrived through the letterbox for exactly this sum. I nearly collapsed. It was from my friends Tom and Jenny. I'd never asked them for money at all. I phoned Tom straightaway. He said they wanted to bless me and encourage me at the start of this new ministry. Naturally, I was overjoyed – and so was he when I told him what I'd prayed the night before.

A few months later, I needed some time to reflect on things so one day I set out into Hampshire and took a walk through a wood just outside Junction 5 on the M3. About half way through the walk, I suddenly felt the urge to 'knock on heaven's door' much more purposefully and dream out loud for the first time about the ideal home I would like to live in, even if I couldn't afford it.

What I dreamt of was a cottage set in amazing surroundings, with woods and fields I could look out on, a large bedroom and a beautifully-crafted study room that could be developed into a kind of sanctuary, with more than enough space for all my resources and furniture, plus a reception area so I could invite my friends and family around to chat and chill out, together with a dining space so I could cook for people and offer hospitality.

I prayed all this, and also that it would be a kind of annexe to a church building and near to church friends. It was a very big ask! I lifted all these dreams to God as I was trekking through a dark wood and the minute I finished, I emerged between two large oaks with sunlight shining in my face as I enjoyed a grand view overlooking fields.

My guidebook told me that to my right was the impressive Greywell House and, unusually for a guidebook, it also highlighted the neighbouring village street. I sensed God speaking to me profoundly and prophetically and within me arose a wonderful hope and, later, a big smile.

Coming out of that tunnel of trees, I felt that God had not only listened to my request, but that he was saying that this place I had dreamt of actually existed. Furthermore, I got a strong impression where it was and that the street mentioned in the guidebook could well refer to my involvement with Street Pastors.

I knew that if this was God's will then nothing could stop it – all I needed to do was trust and hope in His miraculous provision.

The following Tuesday, having prayed more about this situation, I felt prompted by the Holy Spirit to call the vicar of the parish I felt this house might be in, to find out if there was indeed accommodation available. You know what? Not only did he confirm that there was, but his description of what was available (a small cottage owned by his church) precisely matched the description of my dream I had prayed about the previous week. I was blown away.

The lesson I learned?

Dream out loud – at high volume!

So, can I ask you *that question* we spoke of earlier? Why not be brave right now and put this book down and pour out your dreams, hopes and thoughts to God? Being honest with Him is the first step.

Jesus said, "Ask and you will receive." Why not take him at his word? But what of the dreams we have whilst tucked up in bed, fast asleep, when the day is done? Now this is an intriguing topic and, *yes,* God speaks to us through those as well.

I'm sure you can recall some of the strangest, most surreal, most ridiculous, scariest and unbelievable dreams you've ever had, but let me ask you this – have you ever had one that *has come true?*

In 2001, I had such a dream myself. In my dream there I was, wearing my beige combat trousers and my blue U2 hooded top at Christ Church, Barnet, standing at the back of the building. It was at the end of the service in the evening and there was a lady called Heather who couldn't walk properly. I went to speak to her, prayed for her to get better and she was healed. Simple as that. Was this dream from God, I wondered?

Here is the account of what actually took place:

In September that year, I was on the receiving end of some serious verbal persecution from an individual and I simply couldn't take much more of it. At the end of my tether, I attended the evening service at Christ Church and sat at the back.

At the very end of the service the minister, Rev Nigel Taylor explained that there were some encouraging 'words of knowledge' for specific people in the congregation that evening, which the prayer team had sensed God saying to them. He also said that these people were available to pray for 'recipients' after the service.

One of those words had my name written all over it. It described someone who had been unfairly treated, was under persecution and felt demoralised. This described my situation precisely. Within seconds, I had made my way to the chancel and found myself sat opposite two older ladies who were waiting to hear what I'd like prayer for.

Then, a very strange thing happened. As I was beginning to share my troubles with them, all I could think about was whether one of the ladies was called Heather or not! And, did she have pain in her legs? Could she walk? I looked at what I was wearing: a blue U2 hooded top and beige combat trousers. When I'd dressed that day, I hadn't even noticed that I'd put these on!

Everything in me wanted to go for it and pray for one of them – presumably Heather – to get healed. I couldn't seem to concentrate on anything else. But then, I thought, "Hang on a minute, I'm the pray-ee, not the pray-er!"

But the thought would not go away so as I was being prayed for, I thought, "I've got to do this. What have I got to lose?" At the end of the prayer time, they asked me how I felt. I simply replied, "Is one of you called Heather?'"

They were both surprised. And so was I.

Heather was the lady on my right. I took the plunge and told her that I sensed God wanted me to pray for her right there and then to be healed of pain in her legs. I asked if this made sense to her and she explained that she hadn't been able to walk properly for ages and her hips were giving her a lot of discomfort.

Then, another very strange thing happened. As I was praying for her, the fingers on my right hand moved as if electricity was flowing through them. I kept praying, all the while thinking, "What's going on?" I felt warmth and an amazing sense of God's presence.

Eventually, I stopped and asked Heather how she felt. She stood up, overjoyed and praised God. She was healed and walked out of the church without any pain.

I was stunned! But the message was clear:

Dream out loud.

CHAPTER FIVE

One For The Road

Being stuck in traffic never felt so good.

Paul Lewis

Picture the scene

It's Monday morning. 7.26am. You missed your shower, you missed your 'quiet time' and only just had enough space for a sip of coffee – black this morning, since you've run out of milk (again) and you wince as you swallow it, pretending it tastes good, when it doesn't really.

You've simply got to get moving on the road. Another few minutes and it could be curtains, as you know you'll hit the school run. The car's low on petrol, already in the red but yet to show the warning light, so you should be able to make it – you hope.

"Please, Lord, help me," you say. "Just help me get through Monday morning and let the traffic be good …"

Sound familiar?

We've all been there (well, most of us have) and it's not a good feeling, to put it mildly. The weekend (let alone the evening) seems like an eternity away and the sheer weight of the world seems to be pressing down on your shoulders. So what do you do now?

You can't read a Bible (or your devotional notes, or *anything* for that matter, when you're driving), so it's just you and God alone. The good news is, that's actually a really great place to be.

Of course, I bet you're still looking at the clock on your dashboard marching mercilessly onwards towards 8.00am and you may even break sweat in the process … but you'd never admit that to anyone, would you? Of course not. Anyone, that is, except God.

Actually, in reality, this could be a good moment between you and God as you have to be honest with Him and talk to the Lord plainly in a 'needs must' sort of way. But let me ask you this … have you ever asked God to speak to you and spent time listening to him instead? To ask Him what He thinks of you, what He thinks about any situation that's at the forefront of your mind, how you should approach work when you arrive there or even how to cope with that awkward phone call you've been putting off for weeks but can wait no longer?

Don't worry. Remember, God is *for* you and not against you. He really wants the best for you today. Just dwell on that for a minute and let Him in. Then, thank

Him for being with you with you and drive in faith – ask God to speak to you right there and then. Don't put it off (you've put everything else off so far!) – at least try to get this one in the bag before you face the music.

Yes, include everything and *keep your eyes open*. Whatever you do, try not to put God in a box. He can speak to you through anything: backs of vans, road works, registration plates, shop signs, pedestrians, adverts on the backs (or sides) of buses, road signs, posters, banners, scenery ... the list goes on.

Obviously, you've got to keep your eyes on the road. Drive normally and wait on Him.

The situation I asked you to picture at the start of this chapter is one from my own life. It was many years ago, on my way to work at St Mary's school in Hendon, at a time when I was concerned about something in my life. Let me tell you the rest of the story to illustrate what I mean.

As I reached a roundabout, I saw a huge sign by a pub which read 'Chill Out.' It had an impact on me. I felt it was the Lord calming me down and showing me His perspective on things. Encouraged, I drove on to school and over the next few minutes, reflected on what God was saying to me.

Could it be, I pondered, that the Creator of Heaven and Earth is actually saying to me, Paul Lewis, that I should simply chill out on what could (and probably would be) a manic Monday? In a word, yes. I felt it was an encouragement. So far the day had promised only bad news and here was God, suggesting the simplest of solutions. And yet, as I approached my destination, it hardly seemed a simple thing to do.

As I sat there in my car I suddenly found myself wanting to dig deeper into this. I was willing there to be more traffic (there's no pleasing some people, is there?!), just so I could spend more time in the car with the Lord. But it was not to be. I had arrived at school without any further revelation. Just, 'Chill Out'. On the one hand it seemed too simplistic an instruction – easier said than done – but on the other, I sensed that God had spoken and in the car it had already comforted me.

So, I chose to be brave and receive that 'word' for me. Before entering the school, I calmed myself right down and took things at a much slower pace. Perhaps it was supernatural that I was able to do so, or perhaps all I needed was a gentle encouragement from above to put things into perspective, but in the end I actually found I really enjoyed the day. I wasn't running around like a headless chicken. I might have even taught somebody something useful!

The truth is, when you know that God has just spoken to *you* personally, nothing beats it. Just take a look at the promises of God in the Bible – they're full of the joy God takes in us.

The Lord your God is with you, he is mighty to
save. He will take great delight in you, he will
quiet you with his love, he will rejoice over
you with singing.

Zephaniah 3:17

Wow. Just like a loving father who desires to communicate with his children.

Stuck in traffic? Frustrated? You needn't be. Just ask God to speak to you where you're at. What about that van ahead of you? The one that always makes me smile (as it's so biblical) is the AA slogan, *Just Aask*. Perfect.

I could write a whole chapter on some of the answers to prayer I have received through the slogans printed on timely passing vans and lorries, but for now, let me share with you just a small sample of my experience.

In February 2005, I found myself driving up the M11 to Stanstead – the town, not the airport. I was driving to visit two good friends of mine – Jen and Garry Steel. Two adventurous walkers, Garry (Gaz) and I had been discussing and planning our 'great escape' for that the summer for some time: attempting the famous coast to coast walk eastwards across Britain. I was really excited about it, but ... I hadn't yet prayed about it.

Sure, the desire was there and all the logistics could be arranged, but I'd not really involved God on this one much. I could go ahead regardless and pass it off as a grand experience, or I could *Just Aask*.

I guess this is the moment that most of us secretly fear: will God put a stop to our plans and holidays? Many of us panic and think He might say, "No," so don't even bother to enquire. But what if we did?

So, in the car I said, "Lord, do you want me to go on the coast to coast walk this summer with Gaz?" Just at that moment (I'm not joking or exaggerating) a truck flew past me, with the slogan *Coast To Coast* on the back. I interpreted that as a yes!

This wasn't the first time something like this had happened, though. Some months before, I was driving up the M1 to visit my friends Freddy and Ali in Sheffield. It was at a time in my life when I was seriously considering leaving my full-time job as a secondary school teacher (my first teaching post) to pursue a sense of God's calling on my life to be a Christian community worker.

This adventure had been on my heart for some time. I felt in my spirit that God wanted me to have a part-time job at this stage of my life but I didn't really know where or how I should approach this. Should I be a part-time teacher or a private tutor, or should I go for a job as a supply teacher? As I made my way north that day, I asked the Lord.

Just then (again, no exaggeration), a white truck ahead of me came into view. It was advertising some kind of stationery and had the words *The Complete Supply Solution* emblazoned across the back. I smiled. Deep down, I didn't really want to be a supply teacher, but I reminded myself that obedience to God was crucial, and it seemed obvious that He had spoken.

To cut a long story short, I wrote my CV not long after this and sent it to many local schools in the area advertising my services, including supply teaching and it was only by going down this route, that a remarkable opportunity presented itself to me.

After a phone call from a good friend, Peter, I discovered that one of these schools, St Mary's (which, interestingly, was the very first one I'd written to) was looking for a part-time RE teacher to do two or three days a week. Praise God! After praying about it, I believed the Lord wanted me to go for this and when it came to the actual day of the interview, I was the only candidate there!

I went on to teach there for many years, during which time God taught me a great deal and blessed me with many excellent friends and opportunities. It was such a valuable experience that I might have missed had I not been listening and watching on the M1 that day.

On another occasion, whilst leaving Sheffield on the M1 southbound, I asked God to speak to me through vehicles on the road about where my focus should be that week. One lorry on the inside lane read *Kingspan*.

Okay, I thought. What does that mean? Next, a white car in the outside lane shot past me with *King* written on the left-hand side of the boot. I'm beginning to get the picture, I thought and just then, I passed a white truck with the word *Carpenter* written in blue lettering down the side. Okay - message received! I set some quality time aside with Jesus!

Time aside with God

I once asked God whilst on one of my walks in Shropshire what He valued and liked beyond everything else I do. I felt him say, "What you're doing now, Paul." I sincerely believe that. The one thing I'm sure God wants more than anything else is a quality relationship with us as His children.

He wants nothing more than to go heart-to-heart with us, in everything we do, think, say and believe. It is a two-way relationship – just as amazing for us as it is for God. Talking to Him, listening to Him, getting away from distractions and being in that incredible place of intimacy where we can praise Him. Quality time with our Heavenly Father, surrounded by beautiful scenery. Nothing else gets close.

But what if the skies are grey and it's drizzling, windy and cold? Just picture this. Let's imagine it's Saturday afternoon in mid-to-late December and it's that kind of day. You're up against it as you've done no Christmas shopping yet and there's only four days to go until the big day. The world and his wife are out in the streets this afternoon and you know that if you don't make a start today, you're probably not going to get many more chances, since you're back in the office on Monday. The pressure's definitely mounting.

You decide to go with a good friend of yours (who's actually in a similar position, although he's bought *one* present more than you have) and you go for a 'maximum attack' approach. So you pull into the car park, only to find there are no spaces. Frustrated, you exit the gates to park on the road outside and you have only enough money for twenty minutes. What now?

Your mate suddenly spots something in a shop window that he considers perfect for his sister and he says to you, "I'll be back in ten minutes." So you buy a ticket with your last change and sit there. Now it's really pouring down.

Have you ever prayed to God to ask him to help you find great presents for your family and friends? Ten minutes' prayer might not sound like an eternity, but it's certainly nine minutes longer than your 'quiet time' was yesterday! Bring it all before Him. Remember, God cares for you. As the writer says in Proverbs:

Trust in the Lord with all your heart and lean
not on your own understanding. In all your ways,
acknowledge him and he will make your paths straight.

Proverbs 3:5-6

Choose to believe it. Those ten minutes, no matter what the agenda, are precious to God and are actually what you really need. You ask Him to lead you, to guide your thoughts and open the right doors. Above all else, you trust Him. What happened when your mate returned? Well, I'll leave it for you to fill in the rest of the story. It's what we choose to do with those ten minutes that could make all the difference.

In the Bible, Paul encourages us to "pray continually" (1 Thessalonians 5:17) and to "make the most of every opportunity" (Colossians 4:5). Car parks and soaking wet Saturday afternoons aren't exempt from this.

I remember vividly when I took a group of sixth formers on a school geography trip to Somerset. It was on a dreary, wet and cold Wednesday in February. I pulled into a pay-and-display car park in Taunton in the minibus and dropped them all off to nip into town to work on their land-use surveys and questionnaires for their urban project.

This was in 2002, not long after I had sensed God's call on my life for some kind of community work in Barnet. I decided I didn't want to do any shopping, so I sat in the minibus and prayed. I brought everything to Him, including praying about whether this calling was from Him or if I was heading down a dead-end. I prayed that He would confirm His plan.

As I opened my eyes, one of the first things I saw (I hadn't noticed it before), was a huge building off to my right that had enormous white, capital letters on it, saying *Taunton Community Centre*. Again, those ten minutes with Him can change the course of your life.

On the road

Driving can be so much more than just getting from A to B. Let's aspire to make the most of each journey we have ahead of us. The open road this afternoon could be the best passport to new horizons. Who knows what's around the next corner? The journey itself could hold more than you imagine.

If you drive a car or ride a motorbike, let me ask you this: what are your top three drives of your life?

The sense of exhilaration you get on an open coastal highway with the windows down, sunroof open, donning your sunglasses, all accompanied by a pulsating, energetic soundtrack can be absolutely fantastic.

"Okay," I hear you say. "What planet do you live on? This isn't my experience when I hit the road." Yes, I agree it's not always like this. It certainly isn't a barrel of laughs being stuck on the M25 on a Sunday evening coming home from a weekend away going two miles-per-hour behind a sea of red tail-lights. That really is a heart-sinking moment.

Let's freeze there for just a second. Why not use this time to hear from God?

"Yes, but what if the car's crowded, the familiar 'are we nearly there yet?' question gets fired at you twenty times from all directions and I'm exhausted?" I hear you say. God knows exactly what you're going through and you might want to send up a quick arrow prayer in your heart, asking Him to speak to you on the way. Be prepared for anything - including road signs.

These can be great. I know we regularly see flashing yellow lights with *50* and *Slow Down* on them, but has it occurred to you that God wants you to *slow down*? Not just physically there and then, but in the pace that you take life. Must you always be in the fast lane? Are you running to stand still? Or what about, *Tiredness kills. Take a break.*

We live in an age where there's such pressure to get everything done yesterday and cram in so much, some of us even claim we don't have time to eat. Does God really want us to rush around like maniacs? I don't think so. It's not worth killing yourself over saving six minutes at the other end, is it? But it's definitely worth saving your life now and putting those few minutes to good work.

I love the yellow sign they put up at road works, titled, *Start Of Free Recovery. Await Rescue.* It's simply brilliant. We all need rescuing from something or other, even if it's from ourselves. That's what Jesus came to do for us. He can recover our situation and rescue us completely from our mess if we choose to ask him to. Do you want him to?

Reality hits us when we actually see a huge smash on the other side of the motorway. We don't know what caused it but when we see all the flashing lights of the ambulances and fire engines on the scene, and hear the police sirens go off, it's very serious and in some cases, tragic.

Was it someone going too fast? Someone who fell asleep over their wheel because they were exhausted? Who knows, but I believe God does give us signs along the highways of our lives for a purpose and in some cases, warning signs. Why? Because He loves us and wants the best for us.

Have you ever seen the film *Bruce Almighty?* There's a scene exactly like that, where Bruce is calling out to God in his car, asking Him to reach into his life and show him a sign, desperately needing His guidance. God hears his prayer – and shows him some immediate signs. Literally road signs!

How about when the road works end? That moment of euphoria as you are released! Just before you hit the accelerator pedal, take a closer look at the sign. There's someone putting their back into it, with an enormous shovel in their hand, and on their own. Is that you? But look! Underneath that image, there's one short word with three letters - so easy to miss but so vital - *End*.

God might be saying to you that it's the *end* of a period of really hard work and that you need a rest. He's spoken to me through that one a number of times. Go right back to the very beginning of the creation account in Genesis. On the seventh day, God rested. If God Almighty says we should rest (and rests Himself), I think we should too.

On a similar theme, there are service stations. I know what you're thinking: "I'll stop at the next one. I've got enough petrol to last the next three!" Well, that might be the case, but don't turn down the offer of a welcome break. Even if it's just a few minutes to make a phone call or have a quick cuppa, shift down for a moment and do yourself a favour.

Our lives need regular servicing all the time. We're not supposed to run marathons every day and drive till there's no tomorrow. Think back to the accident I mentioned. It's not worth pushing it, is it? Okay, so you admit that the service thing is a good idea. Do you then consider listening to God in the restaurant, when you're tucking into your quarter-pounder with cheese? Why not?

The bottom line is this: Jesus Christ came so that we "may have life, and have it to the full" (John 10:10) and that includes every single journey you'll ever make. Giving him space to talk is not 'downtime' – it could, in fact, be a tremendously uplifting experience.

Enjoy your travels and look out!

CHAPTER SIX

Where Streams Of Living Water Flow

Everyone who drinks this water will be thirsty again, but whoever drinks the water I give him will never thirst. Indeed, the water I give him will become in him a spring welling up to eternal life.

Jesus, John 4:13-14

It sure has been a long drive. You've now been on the road for four hours and you're still an hour or two away from your destination. What's more, it's humid, the air conditioning has packed up, you've exhausted the jelly babies and crisps and you're now winding your way uphill through what seem like disappearing forest tracks, having to negotiate hairpins. And above all else, you're really thirsty. You're desperate, to be honest, for some cool, refreshing water. But where on earth will you find that? It's not as if there's a service station out here – or indeed anything remotely close for miles.

Then, unexpectedly – as if from out of nowhere – a stunning waterfall comes into view (see the picture above). You can hardly believe your eyes.

Immediately, you pull over and step out of the car to behold such an alluring, dynamic, captivating and refreshing scene. The crystal clear pool by the waterfall seems to dance with light as the sun's rays break through the leaves in the tops of the trees and a cool breeze leaps off the gushing waters that pour over the rocks above.

You can't resist this any longer. This is what you've been longing for. So for once, you throw caution to the wind and jump in. Fantastic. It feels like you're breathing in the air of paradise, savouring the taste of freedom and allowing all the weariness of your journey to be washed away by these life-cleansing waters. Simply superb.

What's more, you have no desire to rush away and lose this moment. So there you are, for the next hour or so, enjoying yourself splashing around in the pool and feeling totally alive – completely refreshed, restored and invigorated by such a wonderful experience.

When you finally get back in the car, you feel a different person altogether. Suddenly, the energy and motivation levels are high and your entire outlook on the rest of the journey is positive and enthusiastic. You can't wait to recount your adventure.

The question remains, though, "When can I next immerse myself in an oasis of peace, allowing myself precious time away to restore my soul and give myself the licence to drink from streams of cool, clear, fresh water? When can I get away from it all – for just a moment? When can I escape this rat race?"

This is where we arrive at the very heart of this book: where streams of living water flow, the adventure of walking with God. If you have a bible to hand, take a few moments to read all of John chapter four before we proceed. The conversation Jesus had with this woman at the well is the centrepiece of all I hope to communicate with you.

It was midday just outside a town in Samaria. There was a dry heat and the sun was at its hottest. A Samaritan woman was drawing water from the town's well. Jesus had trekked for miles across the dusty, barren wilderness and was thirsty, so he asked her for some water. She was astonished – not that someone had asked her for a drink, but she was stunned to hear a Jew asking a Samaritan for a glass of water, since Jews never associated with Samaritans.

Furthermore, the fact she was there in the heat of the day, rather than with the other women who would have drawn water hours before when it was cooler, revealed her to be a outcast in her own community. Jesus talking to her was all the more extraordinary.

"Can he be serious?"

"Why – why is he here at midday?"

The sad fact was that everyone else in the village went out of their way to avoid her but *this man* deliberately went out of his way to meet her. Why?

The truth is, this man was more than willing to drive headlong through any political or religious 'red tape' that got in the way and crash through any social or cultural barriers to reach out to her and offer her something that would change her life forever.

She was even more curious now and thought to herself, "How is it he doesn't have anything to draw with? And yet, he's offering *me* living water. That sounds intriguing. What's that? Where do you get that? No-one's mentioned this before!"

Then he said, "Everyone who drinks water from this well will be thirsty again, but whoever drinks the water I give him will never thirst. Indeed, the water I give him will become in him a spring of water welling up to eternal life" (John 4:14).

You can imagine her response, as she told it years later:

"I nearly fell into the well at this point. I'd never heard anything like this before or met anyone like this before in my life. Of course, I said yes. How could I possibly turn down the chance of drinking this mysterious 'living water'?

"Just when I thought I couldn't be surprised anymore (at this point I was expecting him to suddenly produce a bottle of special mineral water from a distant land), he said that I should go and get my husband first, but I told him I don't have a husband. Before I could explain anymore, he told me *everything* about my life.

"I was rooted to the spot. Incredibly, he somehow knew all about my past relationships, broken marriages, my struggles, hurts, rejections, disappointments, heartbreaks, troubles and even the deep longings of my heart. He also knew about my present life, but also seemed to hint at the promised life that was in store for me in the future.

"Talking to this man felt as if time itself had stood still. *He knew me.* There was no getting away from that, but I must tell you, I didn't want to escape, either. It was as if a light had suddenly shone so brightly in my heart and awakened all the dreams I've ever had at once. There wasn't a shred of judgement in his eyes and I felt no need to pretend. He met me exactly where I was and loved me – yes, even me.

"Later, I described the experience as a girl looking into a mirror – and for once, I smiled at the reflection before me. No need to overdress and do myself up to impress, I saw before me the woman I was intended to be since before the world began … like the jewel God had in mind before the creation of the universe. I began to like what I saw. There was such hope for me in those eyes.

"You see, the living water this man offered me was like nothing else I'd ever received before. But this was no ordinary man. Neither was he just a prophet. There was something unique about him. The living water on offer was an honest and joyous relationship with the God of the Universe in a totally personal way. This was the only thing that could truly meet and satisfy the deepest needs I could ever have in life, so that I wouldn't ever have to chase after anything else – or *anyone* else to get satisfaction again.

"The God-shaped hole in my turbulent life of strife had just been filled with an overflow of beauty and love that ran through my veins, like light illuminating my heart, body and soul for all to see. You just have to taste this living water – it is cool and refreshing, it cleanses you from all the rubbish in your life, fills you with hope and joy and what's more, it's *everlasting.*

"Now I know that Jesus offers eternal life to me and to all of us who believe. I'm just so glad he turned up in my village. I'd be lost, otherwise.

"I simply couldn't keep this all to myself anymore. This was the best news I'd ever heard. I felt alive. A new future seemed to open up before me with such gleaming brilliance. It was time to leave that old jar of mine behind. I just wanted to tell everyone in the village. So I did exactly that. 'Come; see a man who told me everything I ever did.' That's what I told them. They believed me. More than half the town came out of the town to meet him.

"He chatted to my neighbours for hours and two of them managed to persuade Jesus to stay at their place for the night. They succeeded all right – he booked in for bed and breakfast for the weekend! We had such a good time. He told us stories all of us could understand and explained parts of the Scriptures that some of us could never hope to understand.

"We actually felt like *good Samaritans*. The person we'd all been waiting for had arrived – the Saviour of the World."

This fascinating story of Jesus meeting the woman at the well perfectly encapsulates the essence of this book.

The streams of living water I refer to throughout these chapters are, in short, those moments in your life where we meet heart to heart with the living God. Nothing else satisfies - like jumping into the crystal clear pool by the waterfall.

Whether it's sitting in your bedroom praying, singing out loud in worship in a Ford Fiesta on the way to work, wandering around your local park in jeans and trainers, seeking guidance for tomorrow or looking out to the horizon on the coast thinking about the future, it's all about quality time with Jesus.

In that same story, Jesus makes the point that it doesn't matter *where* we worship at all – what's important is that when we do worship, it is in spirit and truth.

Just be honest with Him. Tell God what you see and what you feel. Remember, like the woman at the well, He knows your story and where you're up to in it. Where are you right now? Why not invite Him in to your life and ask for that living water?

How do we worship in spirit and truth? This is an interesting question. I believe it is all about being true to ourselves – not being overly religious or pious but simply coming before the Lord as we are. Being honest, showing integrity and acting in faith and trusting Him. Keeping it simple is the best plan of all.

One of the main reasons I love walking in the hills so much is that it offers the perfect environment and setting for tapping into these streams of living water that God is offering us.

I walked a route in Worcestershire recently. It was only a few miles long but featured no less than twenty-seven natural springs (yes, I did count them!). This seemed so symbolic to me of the desire that God has to pour His love and wisdom into our hearts, to restore our souls and renew our minds, so that we are transformed more and more into His likeness.

It is this uncluttered, natural and untamed landscape and a sense of freedom of adventure that sets my heart free from the trappings of an urban existence. It is here that I can truly find myself in 'God's Country', where dreams are a reality, the blue touch-paper of hope is well and truly lit and my whole spirit is elevated to one of overflowing praise and thanks for who He is and what He's done.

Never have I personally felt more alive, invigorated and set free than in these moments. I am always left wanting more. As it is written:

Better is one day in your courts than a
thousand elsewhere.

Psalm 84:10

For the LORD your God is bringing you into a
good land – a land with streams and pools of water, with
springs flowing in the valleys and hills; a land
with wheat and barley, vines and fig-trees, pomegranates,
olive oil and honey.

Deuteronomy 8:7-8

One of the great things about this adventure with God is that this sense of joy and discovery can be shared with family and friends. Some of the best times I've ever had have involved exploring previously uncharted territories in Britain (uncharted by me, anyway) with mates who are seeking those same streams of living water.

The photo above is one of Nick and myself taken in the Brecon Beacons in June 2008. This was an exhilarating journey of spectacular views, fellowship and seeking to press into the heart of God's will for our lives. Definitely one for the album.

I am reminded at this point of the stories C.S. Lewis tells of the adventures of four children – Peter, Susan, Edmund and Lucy in *The Chronicles of Narnia*. Reading these left me totally absorbed by the exciting journey they found themselves thrown into in this magical world. What made these adventures so special was the thought of meeting Aslan, the Great Lion. It had me on tenterhooks throughout each of the stories. I seemed to read faster and faster to reach the bit about Aslan. I was fascinated to see how C.S. Lewis portrayed Jesus, the Lion of Judah.

In the same way that meeting Aslan was so intriguing and illuminating, so it is with engaging heart-to-heart with Jesus. Yes, we will continue to have adventures in life but I believe the real adventure is found in knowing *God himself*.

At the very end of the book *The Voyage of the Dawn Treader*, the children ask Aslan when they are going to return to Narnia. When the disappointing news comes that their time there has now passed, Lucy admits to Aslan that it isn't Narnia she will miss, it is him she'll miss.

The living water that Aslan offered the children was nothing like they'd ever experienced before, just as the living water Jesus offers all of us is nothing like we have experienced anywhere else. And once you've tasted this water, you won't ever want a diluted substitute again.

So just how far will you go to get a glimpse of God? Have you ever sailed to the very end of your soul? It was indeed this desperate cry in my own heart that brought me to meet Christ personally for the first time in my life. I never looked back. I left my old life behind and told everyone I knew what I had done.

CHAPTER SEVEN

A Soundtrack To Your Life

I thought that I heard you laughing; I thought that I heard you sing; I think I thought I saw you try.

R.E.M.

If you were asked to compile an album of twenty songs onto two CD's that best represents your journey through life up until now (your greatest hits), which ones would you choose?

Would they be classic anthems that throw the spotlight on 'champagne' moments of joy and celebration you've enjoyed in your life?

Would they be energetic, uplifting dance tracks that perfectly encapsulate 'mountain top' experiences that you've never forgotten and still, to this day, treasure – and when you hear these songs, you're immediately taken back to that special place? I can almost see you scribbling down the list now.

Or, perhaps they include the ballads? The slow, reflective and melancholy pieces of art that never fail to bring flooding back a whole river of memories from trying times, heartbreak and tears? Would you include them into your mix?

Either way, it would be a fascinating *Best of* collection, which is totally unique to you. That really is the beauty of music. It has that amazing, unique ability to touch that time you had, taking you right back to that very moment – the voices, the smells, the atmosphere and, incredibly, how *you* were feeling in that moment in history. It can be a truly magical experience.

So what makes a captivating piece of music for you? Is it the lush melodies that soar up and down like a roller coaster ride, the rhythm which sets you dancing, the artistic lyrics which seem to speak directly to you (as if they were written especially for you), or is it something else?

The truth is, it's probably an intriguing combination of all of these elements that make up the vital ingredients of the songs that you are likely to include on your album.

I recall vividly my times in the mountains of Snowdonia, in the heart of winter, listening to the soundtrack to the film, *The Fellowship of the Ring*, surrounded by breathtaking lonely beauty. The first time I did that, I felt like I was Aragorn, adventuring through the hills and forests, hiding in the thick fog that enveloped the ridge and jumping the icy streams to outrun a group of pursuing orcs, who were on my tail.

Then there was a more recent time, when I was overlooking the valleys and the villages of the Peak District while listening to the film score for *Gladiator* and feeling like Maximus, leading the charge of an army into the territory beyond, with the wind on my face and the very real threat of rain coming in fast from the horizon.

Even more special, though, are the times that God himself seemed to be speaking to me directly through the music.

In the summer of 2007, I set off to explore the Cornish coast. Before I arrived, though, I brought to God my future timetable in September, inviting Him to guide me and show me the best way I could make use of the time I had each week.

Fifteen minutes before arriving, I thought about Mondays in particular, when I worked alone. I put the

Forrest Gump soundtrack on to the car stereo and pressed 'random', asking God to speak to me. I must have listened to the track *Go your own way* by Fleetwood Mac a thousand times before, but suddenly it spoke to me in a way I'd not heard before. The phrase that hit me more than any other was, "You can go your own way, you can call it another lonely day." Spot on.

Deep down, if I was honest, my biggest struggle was loneliness. I seemed to be working alone for the whole day and, if the truth be known, I would have loved to operate out of a sense of team and community. This led to a very honest discussion with God and actually, punctured the surface of a deeper issue altogether that needed addressing promptly.

Was there a way around it, I asked? The good news was, yes. The Lord showed me the solution and what started with a simple question about how to get through a Monday morning actually ended up dealing with the heart of the matter, which opened up a new way of looking at things for the rest of the week. All from a single lyric.

In a different context, the words God spoken in Genesis 2:18 hold true: "It is not good for the man to be alone. I will make a suitable helper for him."

There have been countless examples of other songs and lyrics God has used over the years, when I have asked Him to speak to me on my journeys. There are far too many to list in this book but here are a selection of 'gold nuggets' which I've written down in my journal, like precious souvenirs acquired on a memorable holiday that made the 'trophy cabinet' in the living room:

The Whole of the Moon (The Waterboys)

This was such an uplifting and invigorating experience. Walking through Sherwood Forest on a cold, cloudy and windy November morning in 2006, I was praying to God for direction and guidance for the future, as I listened to music in my headphones.

I had some idea of where I was heading, but only a few pieces to the jigsaw puzzle ... and then these lyrics hit me:

> I pictured a rainbow, you held it in your hands;
> I had flashes, but you saw the plan.
> I saw the crescent, you saw the Whole of the Moon.
> I was grounded, while you fill the skies,
> I was dumfounded by truth, you cut through lies.
> I spoke about wings, you just flew.
> I wondered, I guessed and I tried.
> You just knew.

See what I mean? I was literally rooted to the spot. Those lyrics were right on the money. God has the bigger picture of my life in his hands. While I may see only a part of the way ahead, He sees the whole of the moon. He knows and He's in control. This was so releasing and freeing!

Driver 8 (R.E.M.)

Hearing God speak dramatically through this song happened whilst driving around my hometown in Barnet. I was under pressure, exhausted and really up against it time-wise to complete a big project.

"What do I do, Lord?" I asked in the car … and these words were sung after I prayed:

> And the train conductor says take a break, driver 8.
> Driver 8, take a break, we can reach our destination.

Fantastic, I thought. I don't need to push all the time. It's time for a break and rest is vital on the journey of life and that's what God wants me to do. Pressure off!

Talk (Coldplay)

Just a few lines in this song are enough to sum up this entire book:

> So you don't know where you're going
> And you wanna talk
> But you feel like you're going
> Where you've been before
> Is there anyone listening?
> But you feel ignored
> Nothing's really making any sense at all
> Let's talk, let's talk, let's talk, let's talk.

I think we can all relate to this. Life isn't easy at all and it can feel like a puzzle so much of the time. There is, though, such an encouragement in this song, and when I first heard it, I did exactly what it said. I talked and talked to God, about everything.

Another poignant lyric, which comes later in the song, is "Tell me how you feel." Hearing this, it felt like God was drawing me close to Him saying, "Paul, I know what's on your mind. Tell me how you feel about this and let's talk. I want to help you."

Those moments that followed were priceless.

Space Oddity (David Bowie)

This one may make you laugh. I was walking through some fields in Hertfordshire and felt that God wanted to talk to me about what I ate for breakfast and how I prepared myself for each day. I had to admit to the Lord that all I had was a coffee before going into work. My excuse? I didn't have time. I knew immediately that this answer wasn't going to win me any gold stars at all.

Spiritually speaking, I felt the Lord was asking me how I'm getting on at putting on the heavenly armour (referred to in chapter three) before I leave the house each morning. Again, I knew my answer might not make the grade.

However, the time that followed was richly rewarding. I felt that God was interested in every part of my life and simply wanted me to succeed in all I did. I felt him encouraging me to take some time before leaving for work, to enjoy a decent breakfast to give me physical energy and to "put on the full armour of God" (Ephesians 6:11) to enable me to be ready for what the day had in store for me.

As soon as I got in the car, I turned on the radio and this is what I heard:

> Ground control to Major Tom,
> Ground control to Major Tom,
> Take your protein pills and put your helmet on.

Yes, I did check the ignition and I knew God's love was with me! Remarkable stuff. I was stunned. Since then, I've enjoyed many a breakfast and quiet time with God before setting out for the day, which has definitely made entering orbit a great deal easier!

Pretty Amazing Grace (Neil Diamond)

I heard this song played on the radio at a time of great difficulty and trial. I was being totally overwhelmed by what seemed like a huge storm of trying circumstances and insurmountable odds.

When I heard these lyrics, I didn't move as I felt God was speaking to me:

Pretty amazing grace is what you showed me.
Pretty amazing grace is who you are.
I was an empty vessel, you filled me up inside.
And with amazing grace restored my pride.
Pretty amazing grace is how you saved me
And with amazing grace reclaimed my heart.
Love in the midst of chaos, calm in the heart of war,
Showed with amazing grace what love was for.

I was brought to tears. What followed was a total change of perspective. I sat in the corner of my room and praised Jesus for saving me. I looked into his eyes of love and remembered his sacrifice for me and that made all the difference. Pretty amazing, to say the least.

Music is simply a wonderful thing. It lifts your spirits, can bring a smile to your face, allows you to emotionally engage with the feelings expressed in a song, stirs you to sing out loud and, like the sun rising to herald the beginning of a new dawn, can illuminate and brighten up a moment in your life, bringing into bloom a beautiful array of colours, which you're only too happy to see.

Take the Underground into London one morning at rush hour and cast your eye around the carriage to see just how many commuters are in need of this diet. It's more than a protrusion of iPods! But that's exactly it – music has a unique way of transporting you to another place and making you feel very different. It's the soundtrack to your journey into work.

Let's not stop at iPod's, though. Whether you're tuning into a radio station on medium-wave lying on the beach to enjoy the tennis commentary at Wimbledon, burning up the highway enjoying your compilation of *Greatest Ever Driving Classics,* playing air guitar in the living room to *Smoke on the Water,* vacuuming to *I Want to Break Free,* pretending to conduct an orchestra in the kitchen to *Pirates of the Caribbean* or singing in the shower to *The Wonder of You,* we live in an exciting age where music is so accessible.

And this is all before I've mentioned the joys of having tickets to sit in the front row of a live performance on stage, being moved by a magnificent opera or West End musical and, of course, let's not forget the excitement of picking up a guitar for the first time hammering out some power chords and nearly blowing the speakers, or grabbing a pair of drumsticks and putting them through the skins in an effort to be heard. It's great fun!

"That's all very well, Paul," I hear you say, "but what's that got to do with God and streams of living water? Aren't we supposed to be talking seriously?"

Absolutely. Let's go and have a look at what the Bible says in the book of psalms. If you've never read the Psalms before, you're in for a real treat. Put away immediately any 'religious' and 'traditional' thoughts you might already have at the very mention of the word, "Psalm." This is certainly no old-fashioned school hymnbook that needs dusting down or repackaging.

These are unashamedly passionate cries from the heart from God's people. These are beautiful songs, honest prayers and deep questions that demand answering. Where are they to be found? That's right: smack in the centre of the bible. And there are 150 of them. More than an album's worth, I think.

So, if you've got your Sword of the Spirit to hand, please put this book down and have a read of a few. You'll get a much clearer picture of what I mean.

Well, which ones did you choose? Was it a plea for help in times of trouble that caught your attention – Psalm 17, perhaps? Or were you drawn to one all about resting in God's goodness, like Psalm 91; or did you go for one that's all-singing and all-dancing? Let's look at the last (but not least) of the psalms – Psalm 150. Here it is:

Praise the Lord.
Praise God in his sanctuary;
Praise him in his mighty heavens.
Praise him for his acts of power;
Praise him for his surpassing greatness.
Praise him with the sounding of the trumpet,
Praise him with the harp and lyre,
Praise him with tambourine and dancing
Praise him with the strings and flute,

Praise him with the clash of cymbals,
Praise him with resounding cymbals.
Let everything that has breath praise the Lord.
Praise the Lord.

Superb, isn't it? So full on and all-out. No half-measures with this. As a drummer myself, this gives me a licence to throw my heart and soul into praising God and 'hit some sixes' whilst playing the drums. If you happen to be a drummer reading this, you'll know exactly what I mean – those annoying nagging words, "Can you *please* play more quietly!?" (This was the polite version) Yes, I know one has to be sensitive and all that, but I've often wondered what it'll be like in heaven praising God. I'll be astounded if He asks us to turn it down a bit.

I sincerely believe that this psalm sheds light on what God desires of us: a full heart, full worship, full everything. Don't hold back.

Think back to the *Dream Out Loud* chapter – that's where miracles happen, when we cry out to God with all our hearts. I recall the account in Luke's gospel when, during the triumphal entry, "the whole crowd of disciples began joyfully to praise God in loud voices for all the miracles they had seen" (Luke 19:37). Then, like party poopers, "some of the Pharisees in the crowd said to Jesus, Teacher, rebuke your disciples!" (verse 39) What is Jesus' response?

"I tell you," he replied, "if they keep quiet, the stones will cry out" (verse 40). That's more than an encouragement to praise him at high volume! I wonder what response you would get if, at a football match, you asked the team's fans to quieten down?!

As we have already seen, Jesus came to give life to the full (John 10:10), and that means we are allowed to enjoy life, enjoy music and enjoy the opportunity of praising Him with everything we have, whether it's with a cutlery set for a drum kit, a hairbrush for a microphone or a tennis racket for a guitar.

Okay, a quick spot of history is needed at this point. Remember King David? Yep, that's the bloke who polished off Goliath. He wrote over half of the psalms, too and is described as a man after God's own heart (1 Samuel 13:14).

Sure, he wasn't perfect, and none of us are, but he gave it his all in pursuing God for all he was worth – singing, playing musical instruments and dancing. He loved God. He wouldn't dare to compromise one bit in his worship of the Lord and sought to give God all the glory. I bet he had a soundtrack to his life.

However, the over-arching theme that I'm drawn to is God's grace. David made some pretty big mistakes, to put it mildly, but always came back to God with a sincere and repentant heart, seeking to be forgiven and restored once more (take a look at Psalm 51 if you need convincing!). There's one scene, though, that says it all about his approach to worshipping God.

Take a look at the scene described in 2 Samuel 6. Again, if you've got the Sword of the Spirit to hand, why not beat me to it and let me know what you think? This scene at the end of the chapter is a celebration of some amazing victories and successes that David was instrumental in: David becoming King over Israel, setting up headquarters in Jerusalem, seeking God for military decisions, having children and managing to defeat the Philistines.

Furthermore, the Ark of the Covenant itself (yes, the one featured in *Raiders of the Lost Ark)*, which represented God's presence with His people, was brought to Jerusalem for all to see. David's response? Here we go:

David, wearing a linen ephod, danced before
the Lord with all his might.

2 Samuel 6:14

Just picture this. Now, this didn't go down too well
with Michal, who was David's wife (and also Saul's
daughter). She'd seen him leaping and dancing around
before the Lord and more than frowned upon this.

When she eventually caught up with him, she said:

"How the King of Israel has distinguished himself today,
disrobing in the sight of the slave girls of his servants as
any vulgar fellow would."

2 Samuel 6:20

But wait for it, there's more. David replies adamantly:

"I will celebrate before the Lord. I will become
even more undignified than this, and I will be humiliated
in my own eyes."

2 Samuel 6:21-22

What a response. Nothing, and no-one even came
close to dictating to him how he should go about his
worship of God. He couldn't give a monkey's! He was
lost in wonder and praise of God's love, mercy, power
and faithfulness and so should we be, too.

Put Him before all else, or *else*. A good challenge to us all, if we want to enjoy drinking from those streams of living water. Nothing else satisfies. It is these streams of living water that I believe David went in search of during his life as a shepherd. Take a look at his life in the Bible if you've got time – he wandered through fields praying to and praising God for all he was worth. He loved journeying with God and the adventure that came with it.

CHAPTER EIGHT

The Adventure Of Walking With God

Where to? Where do I go? If you never try, then you'll never know.

Coldplay

The following extracts are taken from my 'adventure journal', which I have kept since 2003. For the last eight years (at time of publication), I have documented nearly all my journeys and adventures of pursuing God throughout the fields, forests, mountains, lakes and landscapes of Britain.

In addition to describing the beauty around me, I've charted where I'm at spiritually, writing down my thoughts, feelings, hopes, dreams, fears, expectations and desires, together with signs, impressions and revelations that I have felt the Lord say to me along the way.

Right at the start of the Bible, in Genesis, we see Adam walking and talking with God in the 'cool of the day' in the Garden of Eden. The picture is very much like chatting to your friend as you both amble along the beach one afternoon. This is what this whole book is all about: simply walking and talking with God about everything.

This chapter is a selection of entries into my 'adventure journal', into which I scribble down everything I've heard and experienced on my latest journey.

Sometimes, all I have on me is a Sainsbury's receipt to write on, using a borrowed pen from the restaurant owner, but it's been crucial to catch the moment before it escapes forever. Even the most innocuous sign could prove pivotal in making an important decision in life.

Some of the signs have been interpreted straight away, whereas others still remain a mystery awaiting an intriguing solution at a later date. These reflections and impressions have, though, proved to be invaluable further down the line, which have only made sense when looking back.

So, let's take a journey through some of the things God has said to me in recent years:

Edge Hill, Warwickshire
23 September 2005

It all started out so peacefully. Once I'd left the rain and traffic of London and the M25 behind, the skies cleared and there was a fantastic late summer over Warwickshire. The walk began in the picturesque village of Radway – thatched cottages, a village green and an old church. A short walk down the lane gave way to orchards and fields; there was even a surprise meal of blackberries en route (the best I've ever tasted).

As the cloud cleared, I saw one of the best sunsets I've ever seen. Red/orange light streamed through the woods – shafts of sunlight illuminated the darkest corners of the forest. It was incredible. I felt I was Adam in the Garden of Eden. I was talking to the God of the Universe and, as we were chatting, the sunset lit up the wood. I was lost in wonder and praise.

Then, it was seven o'clock. Eventually, clouds covered the horizon and the sun was on his way to bed. I was wearing shades. These were prescription sunglasses so I could see more clearly but it was now getting to the stage where it became much darker if I wore them.

The winding, thickly wooded path continued along Edge Hill. I was walking on a ridge with a narrow path and then, all of a sudden, everything looked much darker. It was. I had to go through it, though. I needed to look for a turnstile on the left into a field to get back. There were noises all around. What was that I heard? "Hello?" I asked. Silence.

Now, I couldn't even see the map in front of me. Had I missed the gate to the left? I hope not. If I went back, darkness would swallow me up. No torch. The path ahead was barely visible now. I carried on. Then, in the corner of my eye, I saw a signpost for a footpath to the left! Was this the stile I'd been looking for? It was! There was even a map on the sign to confirm it.

At the edge of the woods by the field, it was a little lighter. In the field were black cows. That's okay, I thought. As the gate swung behind me, I noticed to my horror the sign on the back of the gate in big, upside-down writing: BEWARE BULL IN FIELD. Oh no.

What would you do now? I couldn't go back in the wood. It was pitch black. So, I skirted along the right-hand edge of the field by a belt of trees and there was a little gate in the opening. I crossed a tiny bridge into another field. There was a cow to my right (twenty yards away). Was it a bull, though? I couldn't see. I continued to walk downhill, following a fence on my right.

I relaxed a bit but then heard noises and more cows (or bulls?) in the corner. There was no path there and it was too dark to see. Oh, I'll duck through the fence, I thought. I touched the wire and, as I did, I got an electric shock. I don't believe it: an electric fence! There was no way out here. Darkness descended.

126

By now, the map was useless – I couldn't see it. My shades didn't help either. If I didn't do *something* in the next ten minutes, I would be trapped for sure. There was only one thing I could do – walk straight through that field of cows and a bull to reach the road beyond. As I started out, one of the cows had come away from the main group and was coming towards me.

Running back wouldn't solve anything. I had nowhere else to go! So I prayed that God would protect me and walked around the stray cow. I had to go through the middle of the herd. I clenched my left fist and fixed my eyes on the gate beyond – if indeed there was a gate beyond. They all stared at me. Keep going. Finally, there it was – the gate. At last!

"What was all that about, Lord?" I asked. I felt Him say to me, "You're made for adventure, Paul. That's the way I made you. Didn't you want an adventure?" I wouldn't have had it any other way, I thought and then smiled. Now, where was my car?

Fownhope and the River Wye
December 16, 2006

Setting out from North London on a beautiful, clear, crisp, sunny Saturday morning, I anticipated greatly some quality time away in Worcestershire and around the Wye Valley.

A pre-Christmas break was just what the doctor ordered. A prize-winning combination of freedom, rest and a change of scenery that make up the vital ingredients of the prescription we all need from time to time. In particular I needed to hear from God – that He would provide and He would guide. To explain why, we need to consider briefly some of the life-changing situations I was facing at the time.

I had just agreed a six-month contract on a cottage, but I had no means to pay, but I knew with all my heart that God had an answer. *He would come through.*

If this was His Will, then I had nothing to fear but everything to look forward to. Trust and faith were what I required. Everything I have, after all, dependent on God's marvellous grace and provision – in all spheres of my life. I don't wish to compromise.

If this weren't enough, a few days after shaking hands on the tenancy agreement for the cottage, I had met up in central London with Paul, my former head of department, who I'd worked with for two years at St. Mary's. I had no idea what would happen next. I simply made the journey to the South Bank to meet up with a good friend, enjoy a meal and catch up and exchange stories.

Within five minutes, he'd told me that he'd handed in his notice to leave St. Mary's and had been offered the job of working at a museum in London. He went on to explain that a fantastic opportunity now existed for me to take the position, if I wanted it: teaching part-time, two days a week. My goodness, I wondered, could this be the path that God wants me to take - not only to pay for the rent of the cottage, but also to continue to use my teaching ability for His glory?

It was a great evening and I left saying that I needed to seek God about this one. I needed that spiritual compass and map, to orientate myself in God's direction and the bearing He had for me.

It was time to hit the hills without further ado and talk to the Lord about this. What did He want me to do? That was my prayer to God in the morning. 'Please show me the way.'

I set off for Hereford to explore. Less than half an hour into my drive, I nearly had a heart attack as I began to pray about whether to go for the part-time RE supply post at St. Mary's School. Incredibly, there was a brown sign to my left with *St. Mary's* written in white letters, and an arrow pointing to it! This was absolutely incredible. I felt in my spirit that this was no co-incidence - God was speaking.

Trying to calm down, I resumed my course on the road and then, fifteen minutes later, driving westwards on the M50 towards Ross-on-Wye, a yellow van shot past me with the words *Pen Tools* written on the back! Again, I felt the Holy Spirit prompting me to notice it, and it seemed obvious to me that it was a reference to teaching. I hadn't even started my walk yet, but God had got there first!

While on the walk, I asked God whether I'd heard Him correctly or not. How could I be sure? At that time, I picked up a trail with deep blue arrows as markings (the colour of the school). It was enough to get my attention. I was walking through a wood. I looked at the name of this wood on the map and it read 'Lea Wood.' I laughed out loud for sheer joy – the bell had rung! That's 'Local Educational Authority!'

Had it been just one thing, I might have been reading too much into it, but with all of this visual evidence from my drive and then the walk, I felt absolutely convinced that God wanted me to take that position. So I phoned the head teacher) the following day to apply for the post - and was accepted. Praise God!

Shoreham, Kent
5 July 2008

I love exploring Kent in the summer. The fields of wheat and barley, the oasthouses and the orchards. This weekend, it was superb. So, I brought my part-time job (as a supply teacher) to God and asked Him to show me the how to make the most of it.

It became apparent quite early on that there were loads of farms on the map; some arable, some pastoral. One was called 'Copthall' and one 'Furnace tae' among others. I got the impression straight away that each 'farm' on the map represents a particular cover lesson to be taught – the reference to 'Copthall' was astounding, as Copthall Sports Stadium is just around the corner from school, where we have our sports day at St. Mary's!

I felt this reference was symbolic of teaching PE. 'Furnace' farm was a farm I'd rather not have seen as I sensed immediately that this signifies particularly tough and demanding cover lessons – literally, a 'furnace.'

There were over eight different farms I'd passed on the walk and I felt this was indicative of the wide variety of lessons I'd need to teach from September, managing a different 'flock' each session.

In addition, there were also several references to 'owls' – owl castle, owl house, etc… i.e. being wise and having a 'castle' to retreat to. So, I need to find a stock room at school to store my equipment, change in and retreat to. This could be the wise move!

The Golden Cap, Dorset
22 July 2008

The walk itself took over three-and-a-half hours and I saved the summit (highlight) of The Golden Cap till the end. This time (after three consecutive days of blue skies and sunshine), it was almost totally overcast, grey and humid. On the outward stretch, there were many signposts that kept pointing to The Golden Cap and it was very tempting to take any one of them – especially since everyone else did!

I resisted, however, and pressed on around the full circuit of the walk. During this time, I asked God what the significance of the 'Golden Cap' meant and I felt this referred to my wife to be – hopefully, in the not-too-distant future! I prayed, therefore, that the timing would be absolutely right and the clouds would clear (both physically and spiritually) just in time for when I ascended the hill later on – in other words, to maximise God's glory.

This really was quite a demanding walk – mainly because it was so humid. As I began the ascent of The Golden Cap, I tuned into *Steve Wright in the Afternoon* at just after 3pm on Radio 2. This half-hour really made me smile with curiosity and wonder, as every song (which happened to be from the 1980's), involved singing about two people coming together.

As I was enjoying listening to these and clambering up the final furlong, the clouds were dispersing rapidly and the grey, overcast blanket of sky soon gave way to blue sky, a sea breeze and full sunshine. When I finally reached the summit, there before me were a couple standing on the edge, admiring the views. How perfectly apt!

The view was absolutely amazing. I could see for miles: out to sea, inland and along the coast. I was in no rush – this was what I'd looked forward to! At the top, I reflected on what had just taken place and believed that God had timed this all perfectly.

Although I could have taken any one of the short cuts available en route, it would have meant that I would have reached the summit too early. It would have been overcast, grey, muggy and humid, with poor visibility, and no sun. Instead, the Lord, I felt, wanted me to experience the 'long' journey with him for all these years to prepare me for meeting the right girl at the appointed time. Although tempting, if I'd 'gone early' up the summit, I may have been very disappointed and unfulfilled.

God's timing is perfect and although I may have had to wait seemingly forever, the views, the journey and the beauty will certainly be worth waiting for.

Leominster, Herefordshire
14 February 2009

After an intense few weeks, jam-packed with everything imaginable, this walk heralded the beginning of a nine-day adventure in half term throughout Wales, exploring parts that I never have done before.

Leaving Barnet early Saturday morning, I barely had enough energy to make it to Wales, let alone do a walk, but I knew that if I didn't at least taste the air of paradise, I'd be missing out on something special. So, I stopped at Leominster for a short hour-and-a-half ramble. I love hearing the voice of God. Within the first twenty minutes, I was completely emotionally and spiritually restored.

Firstly, my identity was affirmed. I remember a walk in the past when I was particularly low; I asked God what He thought of me and how He saw me. I looked up and saw a sign, with a picture called *The White Lion*. This was tremendously encouraging. Two things sprang to my mind straight away – the lion aspect spoke to me of strength, courage and leadership. The 'white' part of this name carried with it a sense of innocence and, through Jesus' sacrifice, being declared righteous in his sight.

So, when I started this walk, guess where it began? That's right – the White Lion Inn! In that moment, I felt God had totally restored, encouraged and affirmed me. What a start to the week ahead!

Secondly, my ability as a writer was affirmed. After crossing a railway and a river by two bridges, I was honest with God by saying that I'm struggling to complete this book – with just two chapters to go (at time of writing). Basically, I'm exhausted and seem to be lacking inspiration and zeal to finish it during this half term.

I asked God to help me – and as soon as I did, I couldn't believe what I saw. There was a car battery lying on the grass ahead of me with the word *Shakespeare* written on it! It was if the Lord was saying that he'd recharge my energy levels and enable me to write creatively and assuredly with this last week to go. Amen!

This wasn't the end, though. This short walk was certainly value for money. I then asked the Lord about whether or not to assemble a team of friends and family to support me with the launch of this book. As soon as I asked, I heard shouts of a football or rugby match being played in a distant field. Sure enough, the binoculars came out, as I wanted to see the action. I was sure the Lord gave the thumbs up to a team strategy!

I then asked God, "Okay, who's on the team? Please show me." Within moments, I was under a bridge and saw, written in massive capital letters, the word DAD. Well, there's one!

WHERE STREAMS OF LIVING WATER FLOW

CHAPTER NINE

X Marks The Spot

We all love adventures, don't we? Whether it's chasing after a getaway car, swinging from a rope over a large chasm, jumping through the flames of a burning building, frantically swimming upriver to escape an impending waterfall, rescuing someone from the clutches of an evil villain or unearthing buried treasure after a lifelong quest, it's in our blood to be a hero or heroine and defy the odds in whatever life throws at us.

I love the big action adventure movies such as *Raiders of the Lost Ark, Star Wars, Lord of the Rings and Pirates of the Caribbean*. They're so inspiring and leave you wanting more. But as great as these all are, the adventure that God has for each of us is infinitely more exciting.

Just think of the ordinary men and women in the Bible who God used in phenomenal ways to change history: Moses to lead the Israelites out of slavery in Egypt, through the Red Sea and into the Promised Land, Paul was taken on huge adventurous journey across the Mediterranean sharing the good news and Esther, who petitioned a King to save her people from extinction.

They were all just normal people like you and me. There's every reason and opportunity for us to be guided and used by God as well, to make a difference in people's lives and the world we live in. Are you up for it?

So let's go on a treasure hunt ...

Whenever my niece and nephew, Mia and Henry, come round to my house, nothing excites them more than a good old treasure hunt. I have this foot-long wooden treasure chest with metal bolts on it that would be fitting in any captain's cabin. So I hide some mysterious treasure within and then get them to close their eyes and count to ... well, sometimes fifty!

Good places to hide it are getting harder to locate all the time. They absolutely love it, whether it's unravelling clues, asking questions, opening up drawers and cupboards or playing *Hot or Cold?*, the quest is just as much fun as finding the treasure itself.

The whole theme of this book is journeying with God. I believe that God is just as interested in the journey we're on with Him on as He is the destination. The sheer adventure of getting to know the Creator of the entire universe and involving Him in all our battles, joys, sorrows, exploits and thoughts is one of considerable worth.

"So what's in the chest?" I hear you ask! Well, you'll have to ask Mia and Henry that one. All I can say is that finding the hidden treasure isn't disappointing. This chapter is all about exploring some of the beautiful environments that God has created for us to enjoy (most of which are not too far away) and also seeking out the reflections of God's beauty and creativity that can be found by adventuring with Him.

Let's seek out these 'hidden' jewels that each landscape possesses and, especially, what the Lord might be saying to us through them. X marks the spot. Don't forget your map and compass! Here we go, then … and when you've experienced walking with God in each one, give the box a tick!

The local park □

This was where the whole adventure began for me. A five-minute stroll from your front door and there you are - open space at last, away from the ringing phone, the television, the news on the radio and all the stuff in your house that fights for your attention. It's just you now, walking in green fields on a beautiful day.

You'll be surprised how different you feel after a few minutes and just how quickly your perspective can change. All the clutter's gone and you can start to think more clearly about things and for once you have the space to reflect - and to pray. God loves to hear how you're doing today.

One of the seemingly hidden treasures of the local park, besides its convenience, has to be its real familiarity. You know the paths well and before long, you've probably worked out a good circuit, which enables you to switch to autopilot mode very quickly.

Not having to think about crossing streams, traversing ridges or clambering up mountains means you can really focus on simply sharing with God all that's on your mind.

The best times are when it's quiet and there's no-one around, because then you're not distracted by dog walkers, children's play areas or that game of football across the field! I bet Jesus had familiar places he could escape to often - whether it was the garden of Gethsemane when he was in Jerusalem or elsewhere, this was time well invested.

So, whether you can spare ten minutes, or three hours 'downloading' everything that's happened to you over the last two months, the local park can be a real treasure island in the midst of a suburban jungle and a welcome harbour from the turbulent waters that threaten to shipwreck your life. He loves to give you that refuge you and I both desperately need.

Snow ☐

However old you are, getting out of bed to draw back the curtains to discover to your total surprise a deep, untouched, white blanket of snow covering the landscape simply never fails to inspire. The winter wonderland carries with it a sense of joy, new horizons and a fresh start to your day.

Adventuring out into the snow is such an invigorating experience. All the landscapes mentioned in this chapter simply can't escape falling victim to its captivating magic and allure. Whether it's carefully making your way over a ridge, ploughing through two feet of snow down your road or crossing the garden, you're exploring virgin territory. Like landing on the moon, the feeling of planting your footprints first, before anyone else, is a pioneering and rewarding endeavour.

Where's the buried treasure now, though? Everything's covered over - how can I possibly find the X on the map in this? The good news is that escapades through snow and ice all convey a tremendous sense of creating the space upon which you can begin to paint a picture of your hopes and dreams on a blank, white canvas.

Snow-covered landscapes present a great opportunity to talk to God about your aspirations of the future and a brilliant invitation for Him to add touches of colour, glistening drops of light and unique reflections to illuminate your way ahead.

The coast

There can be few experiences that are more exhilarating, whilst out walking, than witnessing the always captivating, breathtaking and dynamic panorama where the land does battle with the sea. The enormous and enthralling vista of beautiful sandy beaches, rocky coves hidden amongst towering cliffs, headlands, and a glistening blue sea with the sun's rays illuminating the white crest of each wave crashing against the shoreline never ceases to amaze and inspire me.

Living in Britain, I'm very fortunate to be able to enjoy this spectacular scenery with relative ease. With potentially thousands of miles of coast to explore, this experience is almost inexhaustible and could have you coming back time and time again for more.

Whether it's a hot summer's day with ice cream and beach ball in hand or a late night stroll along a promenade with nothing but the moon and stars above to reveal glimpses of the mystery of the great beyond, the coast has its pearls of beauty in abundance. Among these priceless gems, there are two which consistently strike me:

First, perspective: This is one of the few environments that offers us the opportunity to see for miles to the horizon and can help us see the bigger picture of our lives and what God has in store for us in the future. It's all too easy to get tangled up in the demands of the week. Taking a stroll with the Lord along the coast not only blows away the cobwebs, but can serve to reflect the light of Christ on our hopes for the future.

Second, beauty: While all these environments are stunning in their own right, I strongly encourage you (especially if you've never done this before) to sit outside one morning (or evening) and watch the sun rise (or set) into the ocean beyond. It will take your breath away. Moments like these will stay in your mind forever and give you glimpses of just how beautiful God is.

Fields and meadows ☐

Picture this: Climbing a stile in the corner of a field, you stand amazed at the beautiful view before you. The orange setting sun, emerging from behind a cloud, lights up a moving carpet of ears of corn gently swaying in the breeze. Without a soul in sight, this late summer scene is a joy to behold. This is indeed a rare moment of restoration and peace amongst fields of gold. Nature has a way to join it all together in a beautiful tapestry of His handiwork.

About half of all the miles I've clocked up whilst walking throughout Britain have been across fields and meadows. The enjoyment had in exploring the countryside in this way with such a sense of freedom owes itself to two valuable assets – those of *variety* and *tranquillity*.

Just take a quick look at these opening verses from Psalm 23:

The Lord is my shepherd; I shall not be in want.
He makes me lie down in green pastures,
he leads me beside quiet waters, he restores my soul.
He guides me in paths of righteousness for
his name's sake.

Psalm 23:1-3

Brilliant. This whole book can be summed up in these three verses alone!

God led King David to times of refreshment and relaxation because He knew David needed to escape the trappings of an urban existence in the city. I bet Moses wasn't short of experience in the fields, either, being a shepherd himself for many years. Jesus, no doubt walked through fields on a daily basis – just look at all his agricultural parables, involving mustard seeds, wheat, farmers, labourers, lost sheep … not to mention the parable of the sower!

Next time you're walking through a field or meadow, have a look at what's growing beside you or what animals there are grazing and ask God to speak to you through what you see. Walking like this can be such a refreshing, contemplative and restorative experience to savour.

Mountains

Well, I simply couldn't leave this one out, could I? No adventure would be complete without an epic journey into the snow-covered peaks of one of the most awe-inspiring landscapes on our planet – and it's no prizes for guessing which treasure can be found atop these summits – *awe and wonder.*

A quest into the mountains will literally leave you breathless with exhaustion, speechless with amazement and triumphant with achievement. It's no wonder Jesus spent so much of his time with his Father on mountainsides praying.

This experience elevates your soul and, perhaps more than any other environment, allows you to trace back your journey to where you came from. In miniature, it could be your life story right before your eyes.

The long, winding path up the wooded valley, the precarious ascent along the precipice, the leap of faith needed to cross the river, the perseverance required to negotiate the dark chasm, the strength to carry on and finally, the shout of celebration at eventually reaching your goal ... and what a sight to behold!

The hidden treasure

Well, I can't just finish a whole chapter on seeking hidden treasure without a mention of secret panels, doors or passageways can I?

Imagine you are trying to sell your house. What would happen if one day you were digging out in your back garden when, suddenly, "Clunk." You dig some more and there it is again: "Clunk." Probably a rock or some old tin, you think; that is, until curiosity gets the better of you and you realise the object is a lot bigger than you think.

Suddenly, the excavation takes on a much more puzzling and serious tone than at first. "What on earth is this?" you say to yourself. You look around. No one else is about. You swallow hard. So you mark off the edges. A real excitement and wonder starts to rise in your heart. "Surely not?" you think.

It must be at least a hundred years old. A three-foot long and two-foot wide oak chest with a huge iron padlock protecting its contents. Eventually, after about an hour of digging and carefully prizing out the antique from under the soil, you pick it up to take it indoors to investigate. There's definitely something in there, because it weighs a ton and nearly does your back in.

It's now half past five. You've been there for over three hours, frantically trying to pick the lock without damaging it until finally, "Click." This is it. Now you're sweating with anticipation (and exhaustion) and your heart is pounding with intrigue and fascination at what could lie within.

Suddenly, the doorbell goes. You panic. Now what? You remember that you've got people coming over for a second look at the house. Oh no. You then take one look at your lawn. Yep, there's a massive hole, all right. A million thoughts go through your mind. There it goes again: the bell.

You need the money from the sale of the house and you can't really afford not to answer the door, can you? They're dead set on buying your house. You decide not to move, since they would see you through the window in your front door if you did.

All your life, you've dreamt of an opportunity like this. All the childhood adventures in the woods you had with your friends and the dream of one day telling them, "I've found real buried treasure."

Once again you stare at the chest in bewilderment. "What if there's nothing in it?" you muse. "Am I willing to risk everything – the almost certain sale of my house to a couple who I know are desperate themselves to buy it – for an unknown object in a worn-out old trunk? The thing is, you can't put your hand over to open it, as they will see you through the window in the door and then perhaps come around the side entrance.

Now your mobile phone starts ringing in your pocket. Thank God it's on silent! You let it go to voicemail. Phew. Then, the landline goes. "What if they come around the side entrance?" you think. They'll see you standing rigidly bolt upright against the wall, staring at a chest on the table.

You can't take this anymore. Behind you, to your left, is a cupboard door where you keep all the paint and old tools. It's not big enough, is it? You've never needed to hide in there before! Until now, that is. Turning the handle silently, you creep into the darkness (there's no light) and use the light on your mobile phone to close the latch from within. You feel an idiot. You also feel a hero.

The next twenty minutes are probably the strangest you've ever experienced. You can hear the voice messages from the couple who were outside played back on the answer phone in the hall, expressing their annoyance, disappointment and frustration at you and how badly you've let them down. So you wait another ten minutes.

Have they gone, yet?

After five minutes of total silence, the longest five minutes you've ever experienced in your life, you finally emerge from the closet, your back in agony.

Was it worth it?

Nervous and trembling still, you approach the chest for the second time. What follows next is enough to give someone a heart attack. There before you are golden cups, bowls, tankards, beads and all manner of glistening precious stones that you've never seen before. The evening sunshine shines through the window in your dining room and lights up the chest's entire contents in such a way, you nearly faint!

You are *so* glad you didn't answer the door. These artefacts could well be worth hundreds of thousands of pounds, perhaps even millions. You own the house and the land, so they are yours! You have found what you've been looking for all your life. X marks the spot! This is it.

Remember the pearl of great price?

Again, the Kingdom of Heaven is like a man who
is a merchant seeking fine pearls, who having
found one pearl of great price, he went and sold
all that he had, and bought it.

Matthew 13:45-46

This is a parable Jesus told, which was all about hidden treasure - about earnestly searching for and recognizing the true worth of God's gift to us in Jesus Christ. Although the character in the story I told accidently stumbled across this treasure by chance, the merchant in Jesus' parable purposely sought the treasure, making it his occupation and quest in life.

It is this attitude that God encourages us to take. The rewards are priceless. God has treasures just waiting for you to claim them. They start with redemption, given to you on the cross, but there are more, tailored specifically for you, be it healing, spiritual gifts, vision, joy, freedom, opportunities, ministry, and so on. What would this treasure be for you? What would pursuing it at all costs look like in your life?

CHAPTER TEN

So Beautiful

Your love for me is worth a fortune, your love for me is everything. I guess I'll never know the reason why you love me as you do – that's the wonder of you.

Elvis Presley

Some of the finest moments you'll ever experience are not on camera. This is one of mine: I could never have anticipated this. It was half past eight on a warm summer's evening in 2007. I took a stroll westwards along the coastal path from Lynton to the Valley of Rocks on the North Devon coast. The sun beyond shone a brilliant golden colour and streamed majestically through the branches of the trees, like dazzling headlights on a train emerging from a tunnel, illuminating everything.

I'd done this stretch many times before, but something felt different this time. I walked a few paces more. Unusually, there was hardly a breath of wind. There was no one in sight either and it felt like I had the whole ocean to myself. All I could hear was the gentle breaking of waves against the rocky cliff face below and there, in the distance, in the far West, was the red-orange beauty of a glorious sunset, breaking through the clouds and glistening across the sea.

There was such a profound sense of solace and silence, it's hard to describe. So much so, that when I prayed, I was actually whispering my praise to God and being taken aback by His stunning creation.

Even the footsteps I made became an irritation, so I stopped altogether. As the sun began to sink into the horizon beyond, the clouds reflected its rays with an astonishing contrast – the light, white clouds turned orange and the dark, towering thunder clouds took on a deep red hue, but this wasn't all.

It was like watching an artist at work at the easel; smoothly, carefully and deliberately unfolding a breathtaking scene of such beauty before my very eyes. Now, to the east, an enormous rainbow appeared over the middle of the Bristol Channel and extended further east, where I could only see a fraction of it, before it disappeared through the clouds.

I'd never seen the beginning of a rainbow before (and this one was definitely worth its weight in gold) and to this day I've not seen it happen again. It was a magical blend of awe and silence that moved me to tears. I simply allowed God's beauty to surround me and quietly marvelled at this incredible scene taking shape. Everything else became irrelevant – all I wanted to do was love Him more and be in His presence.

When I eventually set off back to the hotel, I became conscious of some splashing sounds below. "What was that?" I wondered. It seemed louder and more regular than the waves against the cliffs. I wished I'd taken my glasses (or binoculars) as there, fifty feet below me, were two dolphins jumping excitedly in and out of the water barely any distance from the rocks. This was some scene.

The whole experience lasted an hour and had such a refreshing and transforming effect on my soul, it felt like I'd just witnessed a stunning reflection in a mirror of a plethora of wonderful characteristics of God – beautiful, awesome, joyous, captivating and delightful.

When I finally returned, I felt altogether different. Before half past eight, there had been many things weighing on my mind. I was frustrated, downcast and exhausted. By half past nine, however, my entire spirit had lifted. I felt lighter, happier and at peace. I'd encountered God in such a beautiful way and it felt like liquid love was being poured into me. My whole perspective had changed. The Son had shone with such brilliance that he left me utterly awe-struck.

Praise him, you highest heavens and you
waters above the skies.
Let them praise the name of the Lord,
for he commanded and they were created.
He set them in place forever and ever;
He gave a decree that will never pass away.
Praise the Lord from the earth,
you great sea creatures and all ocean depths.

Psalm 148: 4-7

The heavens declare the glory of God;
the skies proclaim the work of his hands.
Day after day they pour forth speech;
night after they display knowledge.
There is no speech or language
where their voice is not heard.
Their voice goes out into all the earth,
their words to the ends of the world.
In the heavens he has pitched a tent for the sun,
which is like a bridegroom coming forth from his pavilion,
like a champion rejoicing to run his course.
It rises at one end of the heavens
and makes its circuit to the other;
nothing is hidden from its heat.

Psalm 19: 1-6

You may have spotted that I said my experience in Devon was not caught on camera, and yet I included a photo of a stunning sunset on page 153. In fact this was taken a year later at Land's End. This was the furthest West that I could possibly go in England. I sat there for hours savouring every moment of that sunset and was completely blown away by its beauty. That moment *was* caught on camera and will live with me forever.

The psalms in the bible are full of praise for God: his awesome majesty, unconditional love, compassion, beauty, righteousness, holiness, faithfulness and so much more. If you have a moment to explore some of these wonderful prayers, supplications, songs, poems and cries from the heart, you'll undoubtedly be struck by how passionate David was about the Lord.

We looked closely at David in chapter seven and saw that he wasn't perfect by any stretch of the imagination (and he knew it, too), but what is so encouraging about him is how he pursued God with all his heart. In just about every situation he found himself in, whether it was seeking military guidance, direction in leadership or asking for wisdom in making vital decisions, he was genuinely enquiring after God in a personal and intimate way.

I bet he walked and talked with God in the fields, forests and wilderness where he lived, too.

David, however, wasn't simply a man who only sought God if he wanted to solve a problem. David loved God and it was this that made all the difference. Why not read for yourself the Psalms and read out some of the songs and praises he gave to God.

He clearly marvelled at God's beautiful creation, but also worshipped the Lord for who He was, being joyfully swept away in a wave of overflowing gratitude and amazement at God's awesome character and ways.

Do we want to fall in love with God like this? I hope so! I believe this is the key to everything and the very reason we were created, to be captivated by an intimate relationship with the creator of the universe.

Let's not delay any longer. Let's look at this from an eternal perspective. Having this kind of honest and freeing relationship with Jesus Christ not only transforms our very lives here on earth now, but also has major far-reaching implications.

The promise of eternal life in heaven with God himself is something I can't wait to experience. I desire so much to see God face to face. If a sunset, a mountain range covered with snow or a perfect reflection of a forest in a clear lake astounds me now, how much more will I be astounded by what awaits me when I'm called to be with Him forever?

Walking isn't simply a quick-fix tool kit to make us feel better. I believe the whole experience can serve to shift our entire perspective away from ourselves, help break the shackles of a cluttered existence and bring us out into the open, where we can stand amazed at God's magnificent creative masterpieces that reflect his glory.

Being completely caught up in the awesome wonder of God is simply indescribable. It really is an adventurous voyage of discovery we can all have that transcends anything else we've seen or even imagined.

Whether Elvis Presley had this in mind when performing the song *The Wonder of You,* or Baker Knight when he wrote it, I'll never know, but when I listened carefully to those lyrics, my thoughts were quickly drawn to so many of God's characteristics and ways.

When I've stopped to consider just what Jesus went through on the cross to save me from my selfish, sinful ways, I'm left dumbfounded by his grace, overwhelmed by his mercy and utterly transformed by his love. I'm free!

It is no surprise, therefore, that countless people throughout the course of history have composed songs, written books, sung hymns, painted beautiful ceilings in chapels, hand-crafted sculptures, penned poems, directed films, narrated stories, acted out entire plays and painstakingly constructed architectural masterpieces all to honour God for who He is.

I think the hymn *How Great Thou Art* sums it up perfectly and capture the entire essence of this book. I would encourage you to read the whole hymn but for now, just take in this excerpt:

> O Lord my God! When I in awesome wonder,
> Consider all the works thy hand has made,
> I see the stars; I hear the mighty thunder,
> The power throughout the universe displayed;

> And when I think that God His Son not sparing,
> Sent Him to die – I scarce can take it in,
> That on the cross my burden gladly bearing,
> He bled and died to take away my sin:

> *Then sings my soul, my Saviour God, to Thee,*
> *How great Thou art!*

One of the most memorable experiences I've had when trying to comprehend the utter vastness, majesty and eternal qualities of God occurred while taking a peaceful stroll at night along the beach at Sheringham in North Norfolk. It must have been nearly midnight and there wasn't a soul in sight.

Upon reaching the end of the promenade where the lamp-posts bid me farewell, the scene dramatically transformed into one of breathtaking beauty. Not a cloud in the sky. There I was, under a blanket of stars, unveiled in all their majesty across the night sky, with the moon illuminating the sea accompanied by the relaxing soundtrack of waves gently lapping at the shore. This was so beautiful.

The outflow of being intimate with God

Jesus said that he'd come to give us life to the full and he meant it. One of the age-old questions and mysteries that I (and perhaps countless others) have wrestled with for years has been, "Why am I so exhausted all the time?"

Why is it that I seem to resemble a pot with holes in the base? The very second that water arrives in the vessel, it seems to disappear just as fast in so many different directions through holes at the bottom and, as a consequence, I end up totally drained, utterly spent and frustrated.

"But surely I need to give out to all these people all the time?" I ask. "How can I avoid burnout?" This was a regular question I used to throw at the Lord in desperation. "What's the answer?"

One Sunday evening, a visiting speaker at a church shared openly with the whole congregation precisely this conundrum. I sat bolt upright and listened. I didn't move. I really needed to hear this.

The picture he described of the vessel with the holes at the base made perfect sense. My 'pot' was never full. I just seemed to give out all the time. He went on to explain that the truth is, everyone wants a piece of you. This could be your husband, wife, boyfriend, girlfriend, brother, sister, parents, children, friends, work colleagues, but also the 'demands' of sport, music, hobbies and service to others.

In a sense, we all have a divided heart and are consequently pulled in many directions all the time, and therefore drained of energy. Many of us can't say no either. So what's the solution?

He went on to say that God wants us to give Him an undivided heart – a heart that desires Him more than anything or anyone else and that when we dare to spend quality time with the King of Kings, He will completely fill our 'pot' - more than fill it - so that it's overflowing. Let's look at God's Word here:

> Give and it will be given to you. A good measure,
> pressed down, shaken together and running over,
> will be poured into your lap. For with the measure
> you use, it will be measured to you.
>
> **Luke 6:38**

Therefore, when we give out to others, we do so having being first filled by God, so that the overspill of God's love pouring into us can't help but soak others we come into contact with. Rather like a fountain of living water.

This is not a performance on our part, but an outworking of His love, grace, mercy and power. Ironically, another Elvis Presley song comes quickly to mind here: *Can't Help Falling in Love With You.* If we can't help falling in love with God, that's the best place to be. It will transform absolutely everything. You'll discover just how beautiful God is. This is a voyage of discovery that will last forever.

Finally, Jesus reinforces this by encouraging us that he is the vine and we are the branches and, "apart from me (Jesus) you can do nothing" (John 15:5). Let us encourage one another to draw streams of living water from the true vine so that we can produce some mouth-watering, long-lasting fruit for His Kingdom, so that many people's lives will be radically transformed.

This is exactly how it happened for me as I met Jesus myself in 1994.

CHAPTER ELEVEN

Last Orders

Almost ten years before I began writing in my journal, I was sat upstairs in the *Tally Ho* pub in Finchley talking with my mate, Steve.

We've been friends ever since the beginning of secondary school and we were in the Barnet Schools' Symphony Orchestra together. He was scraping away on his cello, while I was happily banging away on the drums. We remained good friends after leaving school and through the rollercoaster of a ride of university.

This conversation over a drink, though, was the most important one I've ever had. I'd been thinking about Christianity quite deeply over the previous few months. So much had recently happened in my life. In late August 1994, I asked Steve this question: "If I repent and believe that Jesus died for my sins and that he rose again, and I put my faith in him, does that mean I'm saved?"

At that precise second, the bell for last orders rang. There was no mistaking it. This was more than just a coincidence. Both he and I looked straight at each other and sensed that God agreed. It was an *eternal moment* and one that I'll never forget in an instant. I knew that Jesus had loved me and had died for me. He had saved me. It was true.

Things didn't stop there, though. Within a few weeks, I'd returned to Leicester University a very different man. My friends noticed that there was something different.

One Friday evening in Leicester, I met up with a friend, Debbie and told her everything that happened over the summer – how my life had been completely transformed and that I was a Christian. She was overjoyed and we began walking back through Victoria Park to our respective houses.

What happened next was extraordinary. I suddenly felt a tangible 'fire' burning in my heart. I'd never experienced such a feeling in my life before. It was incredible and carried with it a tremendous sense of freedom, joy, peace and contentment. It didn't go out either!

In fact, this fire lasted for about two weeks. During this time, life itself took on an entirely new perspective. So many 'chains' that I'd been imprisoned by for years fell off. Fears of rejection in relationships all evaporated, worries of not getting a good enough grade at university disappeared, like a mist being burned away from the sun.

Intellectual arguments that I'd once held in opposition to believing in God just simply disintegrated and I saw them for what they were. I even laughed at them. I actually felt loved for who I was. I began to pray. It felt weird at first, but so releasing, that I could ask God for anything. I saw nothing as a barrier anymore.

The future suddenly opened up like the first chapter of an absorbing, incredible adventure which was unfolding before me.

A few days later, I saw Debbie walking through the park on her way to a geography lecture. I raced over and told her what had happened – especially about this strange fire that was burning in my heart. She smiled and said, "Paul, that's the Holy Spirit."

"The *what?*" I replied.

She had about five minutes before the lecture started to explain who the Holy Spirit was. Everything slotted into place. Not long after this, I spotted an intriguing passage in the Bible I hadn't seen before. If you've got your Sword to hand, have a quick look at the Emmaus Road encounter in Luke 24:13-35.

Once you've finished, just rewind a bit to verse 31: "Then their eyes were opened and they recognised him, and he disappeared from their sight. They asked each other, 'Were not our hearts burning within us while he talked with us on the road and opened the Scriptures to us?'" How amazing is that?

Very soon, I began to want to seek out places where I could pray to God without being constantly distracted. The only room in my (shared) house that vaguely offered me some solace was the bathroom. I soon had a reputation for taking ages to have a bath!

I needed to find a place that wasn't so confined, though. It was obvious - go for a walk through the park. I could pray anywhere, I figured, so Victoria Park seemed perfect.

Most of my early prayers were asking for help to get through my finals at university. The end of my previous year had been almost a total write-off and I was in danger of failing altogether. So I prayed that the right questions would come up in my exams and that God would guide me and help me to revise and remember all I needed to.

Never before have I felt so assured, relaxed and optimistic about exams! The results were staggering. From a position of near failure one year earlier, to seeing my name on the board outside the faculty with 2:1 attached to it was more than I could have hoped for. Thank You, Lord for hearing my prayer.

So, this was how all this walking and praying really started. And since then it has only got better and better. No walk is ever the same twice. Just try it and see.

There is a time for everything, and a season
for every activity under heaven.

Ecclesiastes 3:1

The changing seasons in our climate can sometimes uncannily mirror the seasons of our soul. The early sunrises at dawn in the summer can paint a picture of a

166

breathtaking new beginning. The captivating reds and rustic colours of autumn leaves may reflect a beautiful change up ahead. Perhaps after a long, dark winter, the sudden burst of daffodils and bluebells into bloom on the first day of spring may echo the hope of the dream you've spent all your life thinking about coming to life.

It's time now to begin writing your own adventure. Like Frodo and Sam in *The Lord of the Rings*, we all have a purpose and destiny in life and we all have a book in each of us that's just waiting to be written and read: Your adventure with God. I'd love to hear about your experiences on your journey.

I've only scratched the surface of some of the ways I believe God speaks to us in life – what about through family, friends, colleagues, movies, books, buildings, dreams, visions and supernatural means? In this book I have tried to share only the ways God has spoken extraordinarily to me as I have travelled on my journey with Him but He can and will speak differently to you.

And I'd love to find out how you get on.

The wonderful thing about God is that he is beyond our understanding and full of surprises. So, in the words of U2: "Get on your boots!" I'd like to encourage you to go on two walks in the next month to get you started. Don't run before you can walk – choose places that won't be a burden to get to. And when you go, start talking with God about anything and everything. Share your life with Him, ask questions, dream out loud. And most importantly, expect God to answer, in both subtle and dramatic ways. Maybe He will speak to you in ways I have described – through vans, signs, scenery, situations and music. Or maybe it will be another way.

Whatever happens, record your experience. To help you do this I have included two simple templates on the next two pages: one for a walk alone, just you and God; the other for a walk with a wider group. I hope you find these helpful.

Enjoy!

SCENE ONE: You and God alone

Date:

Location:

Questions that you asked God / things that you spoke about:

Any answers to prayer you may have sensed (impressions, pictures, signs, things you saw, etc.):

SCENE TWO: The fellowship

Date:

Location:

Questions that you asked God / things that you spoke about with your companions:

Any answers to prayer you may have sensed (impressions, pictures, signs, conversations, things you saw, etc.) or words given to you:

You're probably thinking, "Is that all the space I get? I can't possibly squeeze it all in!" Then again, that's really great to hear, if you *are* thinking that. Maybe it's already time for you to get hold of your very own 'adventure journal' and get the ball rolling. You'll be surprised by just how much you write!

It doesn't have to be a leather-bound piece of parchment, hundreds of years old, that Indiana Jones would have been proud of – even a petrol receipt will do for the moment. Before you know it, you'll be writing your own book. I once told one of my classes at St. Mary's School that I was in the process of writing my own book. They looked very surprised and there was a short silence. Then, someone said, "Can anyone write a book, Sir?" I laughed. "Well, if I can do it, then anyone can," I replied.

I realise that throughout the course of this book, I have focused almost entirely on the aspect of walking alone with God. It's not that I've purposefully chosen to be anti-social but I sincerely believe that it is this intimate relationship with God that is pivotal.

I have had many journeys and adventures with friends and family over many years. Many have been fruitful and I have enjoyed immensely the feeling of sharing the experience of walking with God with others. The photo overleaf is one of Gaz and me trekking through the Lake District in July 2005 on our way to finding the youth hostel somewhere in the far distance. This was such an adventure.

It really is encouraging to see the joy, wonder and sense of anticipation on the faces of those I travel with.

Two walks on Stanton Moor and Padley Gorge in the Peak District with my friend, Freddy, gave him the inspiration to write a whole fictional book, appropriately called *The Lost Story*[2], based on such an invigorating and enriching experience: the journey of discovering God.

On another occasion, I'd taken my brother Rob, with his wife Kim and their two children, Mia and Henry, together with friends Emma and Asha on what felt like an uncharted expedition through a myriad of cascading waterfalls amid a dense cover of forest in the Brecon

---

[2] The Lost Story: The Scroll of Remembrance, by Freddy Hedley, was published by Emblem Books in 2010.

Beacons, which was nothing short of absolutely exhilarating.

So let's imagine that bell for last orders rings out again. You've got what you need now for the journey ahead.

One of the reasons I decided to write this chapter is to encourage you to break away from the 'bank holiday experience'. By that I mean only ever going out on a sunny, warm bank holiday Monday in late May or August and thereby running the risk of never experiencing the hidden gems that the Lord can use to speak into to our hearts as we journey with him through life.

So, let's not be hedgehogs, hibernating in the shadows any longer. Your journey with Jesus will take you through all the seasons, ranging from the enchanting beauty of a majestic sunrise through a valley of daffodils in late spring to the warm red-orange glow of a sunset behind the snow-covered hills in the bleak mid-winter. Go for it!

CHAPTER TWELVE

What About February?

But February made me shiver, with every paper I deliver. The bad news on the doorstep; I couldn't take one more step.

Don MacLean

"What's all this about?" I hear you ask. The inspiration for this chapter came in February 2008 on a walk through the Cotswolds with a good friend of mine.

We were discussing how seemingly difficult it is to motivate oneself by heading out into the hills in the early months of the year, but how glad we were that we had made the effort. After the way God spoke to both of us on this adventure, and the scenes we captured with the camera, we felt like we'd discovered the proverbial pearl in the oyster.

The irony was that it turned out to be the sunniest February on record. Despite this, I've specifically chosen February as a month in the year that can often present us with enough barriers to dampen our spirits and can often result in keeping us inside for far too long. The frustration of being chained to our indoor world can make us feel like a bird trapped in a cage, desperate for the sun, the wind beneath its wings and the freedom to fly wherever it wants to go.

But we often get so used to our cage that we forget what it's like to breathe the fresh air of the paradise we were used to. We may even go as far as thinking those steel bars are there to protect us from trouble. Without realising it, we soon get suffocated.

It's true, isn't it? By February, the festivities and celebrations of Christmas and the New Year's party with family and friends are now all but distant memories. Summer is a word you've not used for ages. It gets dark at half past four.

You look outside and see grey skies once more with the rain lashing at your window-pane. All you want is a bottle of milk from the newsagents down the road, but everything seems like such an effort. It's cold as well, but you begrudgingly reach for your coat and look for some loose change. Most of that's gone, too. Your financial picture seems as bleak as the scene that greets you as you open the door.

I hope you see where I'm coming from. I've tried to paint the most depressing picture I can, but this is where the rubber hits the road. So what about February, then? That's the question.

Is this, then, a month when we just have to grit our teeth and get through it, or can we dare to believe for a moment that the God of the universe wants to come and meet us where we are and, like rays of sunshine, burst through the clouds in our hearts and light up something truly beautiful, transforming this month into one of incredible hope, brightness and opportunity? This is what it boils down to. Remember, He loves you and he has the best for you. We just need to ask.

Think back to the woman at the well. Did she realise that her real need was for the living water that only Jesus could give her? She was thirsty and needed to drink. Jesus offered her living water. Now let's flick back to the scene I described on the previous page. Most of us have been there and, if we're honest, the last thing we want to do is take a walk in the rain!

Surely, there's a DVD that might cheer us up a bit, a magazine on the coffee table that would make us laugh? Or how about surfing the internet or playing a computer game for an hour? Surely that will help us escape where we're 'at'? Let's lose ourselves in a virtual world for a while and forget about paying the bills.

The challenge is this: which fountain do you want to drink from? Do you want the living water that Jesus offers you or do you settle for something else? The American singer, Plumb, sang, "There's a God-shaped hole in all of us and a restless spirit searching" (in her song, *God-shaped Hole*). This lyric encapsulates the desire

God has put in all of us since we were created. The way the bible puts it is even more striking:

He has made everything beautiful in its time.
He has also set eternity in the hearts of men.

Ecclesiastes 3:11

A not-too dissimilar scene to the one I've just described has happened to me. Everything in me said, "Stay at home," but there was this still small voice calling me out.

The cage has its lock on the inside. I looked at it again. Within moments, the waterproof jacket and trousers went on – and the beanie for good measure! I didn't care what the weather was doing, nor if I got soaked. I desperately needed and wanted time with my Heavenly Father. In Sweden, they have a saying: "There's no such thing as bad weather, just bad clothing choices." It's all too easy to come up with any excuse to avoid leaving the house but it could be a half-hour that just might turn your day around.

Some friends and I were staying at Lizzie's house in Somerset at the time and a number of them had gone out for a few hours. Into the mist and rain I ventured, and proceeded to follow a lane through the village out into the countryside. I got so carried away talking to God about everything that was on my mind, I didn't even notice that it had stopped raining!

I passed countless farms, fields and houses and must have walked for miles. I loved it. The whole landscape and weather carried with it a mysterious veneer that I found totally absorbing. I asked the Lord to speak to me and within minutes, it seemed like my whole perspective on the day, the week ahead and the month were completely transformed. I just wanted to walk forever. My whole spirit was lifted and I had the energy, hope and excitement to face the weeks ahead. One 'phone call' to the Lord changed it all.

For me at that moment, this was where the streams of living water were in full flow. I was an empty and depressed vessel inside, but was soon transformed into an enthusiastic, full and hopeful chalice, having had a much-needed pit-stop.

As my friend Nick felt the Lord say to him: "Pursue me into the wilderness and I will let your heart run wild."

CHAPTER THIRTEEN

Can You Cut It?

This is the face of letting go.

James Blunt

Well, this is the million-dollar question, isn't it? I thought the last chapter was to be the end of the book. I finished it in February of 2009, sat back and celebrated with a glass of champagne. Five years of adventuring, writing and editing had come to an end. Or so I thought.

You may have reached the end of the previous chapter and thought to yourself, "That's all fine for him - he's single, has a job, drives a car and has virtually every weekend available to shoot off into the mountains and spend quality time with God. How can I relate to that?

"My circumstances are totally different," you may continue, "and I struggle to get anytime to myself. I'm lucky if I get five minutes in the shower, let alone a day to myself. I have two children to support and work three jobs to make ends meet. How does that work, then?"

Well, since completing the last chapter, my circumstances have changed dramatically. On the 6th September 2009, I met Julie. It was as if our hearts and minds met. She was absolutely beautiful. One week after our first date on the bank of the River Thames, our relationship was moving at quite a pace and everything was so exciting.

Two weeks later, I met her three adorable children. By the end of half term, we'd been on days out together and were spending so much time enjoying this new adventure. In six weeks, I'd gone from a single man who'd 'flown solo' in life for seven years to a potential step-father of three! Indeed, in a few months we were engaged and we married in July 2010.

This is where the rubber hits the road. All the work of the previous twelve chapters - and indeed, all the time I'd invested in pursuing intimacy with God throughout my walk with Jesus has now given me the opportunity to cut it in this new phase of my life.

Becoming a husband and a step-father of three is certainly the biggest challenge of my life so far. I suddenly entered a whole new arena. It was like going from playing Sunday league football one week and then being picked to represent England the next.

Many friends of mine who are married with children had told me that getting time alone in a family setting whilst working a job is nigh on impossible and that your life isn't your own anymore. This was a serious chestnut to crack.

"If you find an answer to that one, let me know," said my friend Dave. Game on, I thought.

Being a single parent is such hard work. I had such admiration for Julie. "How on earth have you managed?" Even before we were married, whenever I had the privilege of spending several days with Julie and the children, I quickly realised that time on your own - and more importantly, time with God – becomes extremely to find. Now that we all live together, I know it even more!

But then I ask myself the crucial question: "Just how precious is that water?" If the streams of living water that Jesus has poured into my life have more than sustained me all these years, how can I afford not to drink from the well? Just how desperately do I need to drink this living water? This is the heart of the matter.

I know that without this intimate time with God, I will have nothing left to offer. I would be like a car with an empty tank about to embark on a long journey; I would be a secondary school teacher who goes into a challenging school with no sleep the night before; I would be a boxer in the ring, about to fight for the title who hasn't eaten a meal for the last 24 hours; I'd be a ship with a mast without a sail. I would be finished.

The bathroom

"What on earth has the bathroom got to do with all this, Paul?" I hear you say. Have a think back to the chapter X

Marks The Spot. Remember we explored all the wonderful environments where you could walk with the Lord, to unearth all manner of beautiful and reflective treasures as you journeyed with Him through his creation?

"Oh yes, I remember now, but I'm sure there was no mention of the bathroom. Was there?" I've heard it said that every man has his cave. Whether it's a shed at the bottom of the garden, an office you retreat to or even a cupboard that you hide in - wherever it may be, is there a quiet area in the house that you can escape to, in order to find solace?

I know what you're thinking. You're probably laughing to yourself, "Welcome to the real world, Paul! There's no escape now with three children running round the house. You can't just shoot off into the mountains and sit peacefully by a quiet lake now, can you?" No, you're right. I can't. I can't and don't want to bury my head in the sand and absolve myself from my responsibilities as a step-father.

But wait a minute – I need Jesus. In fact, I need him more than ever now. I think I'm finally beginning to understand why the Lord got up so early. Why was he out and about in the fields before anyone got up? He needed intimacy with his Father. There was no other way he could have done what he did. He loved His Father so much and he would do anything he could to get precious time with Him.

So, the bathroom has actually become my secret haven. I can lock the door and run myself a bath and pray - just talk to God about everything. This is where most of my praying started at university. It's as if it's gone full circle.

Try it and see for yourself. Lock the door, turn off the lights and begin to talk. Half an hour with the Lord like this suddenly begins to transform everything - and besides anything else, I'm cleaner and fresher than I was before! But more to the point, I feel rejuvenated in my spirit. I feel I have given God my burdens, offloaded my needs, asked Him for divine help, sought His face, gained His wisdom, enjoyed His presence and felt joy.

I love Jesus. This living water that he offers is more vital to me now than ever before. What's more, I can pour out this water that he offers into the lives of Julie and the children. I can allow Him to work powerfully through me. The bathroom has become one of the finest caves imaginable.

The cupboard

"Oh, Paul, this is ridiculous! Is it really that bad?" Please allow me to defend myself. Before you jump to conclusions, no, I'm not hiding in the cupboard upstairs, like a game of hide n' seek.

Look again at those last three words of the previous sentence. What do you see? "Ok, Paul, so if you're not hiding from everyone in the house, what are you doing? You haven't discovered a magical wardrobe upstairs that leads to another world, have you? You haven't found Narnia, have you?"

Actually, a cupboard does exist - but not at home. It's at school. I see you put this book down immediately in astonishment and utter bewilderment. "You mean, you hide in the cupboard at school?" Yep. "You're mad."

It's not as mad as you might think. Anyone who's ever taught in a nursery, a primary or a secondary school or worked with large numbers of children of any age and at any capacity, knows that it's very hard work. You can't just hide behind a computer screen and pretend the kids aren't there. After several hours on the trot, you need to seek out that quiet area.

I currently teach four subjects - Maths, PE, RE and Leisure and Tourism, so I have a good case for needing some space to keep all my diverse materials together. I found a small storage room on the first floor that is probably no bigger than your bathroom (see, it's the bathroom effect again). It is full of old papers, filing cabinets and all manner of novels, study guides and old exercise books. It doesn't sound particularly pleasant, does it? But it's brilliant.

Sure, it doesn't have a red carpet or have chandeliers hanging from the ceiling, but it's a place I can not only change in (from a suit into a PE kit), but more importantly, sit down for a moment and quiet myself before the Lord. Five minutes of this is worth a thousand elsewhere.

Look at this verse from Matthew:

> But when you pray, go into your room, close the door
> and pray to your Father, who is unseen. Then your
> Father, who sees what is done in secret, will reward you.
> And when you pray, don't keep on babbling like pagans,
> for they think they will be heard because of their many
> words. Don't be like them, for your Father knows what
> you need before you ask him.

Matthew 6:6-8

Did you notice the words, "reward you?" For years, I've never spotted that until now. If that's not a motivation for prayer, then I don't know what is!

The cellar

"Oh, Paul, is it really that bad? What's wrong with your bedroom? Now you're going underground!" When Julie and I married on the 24th July 2010, we moved into a wonderful house (this was such an answer to prayer - you'll have to wait to read about this in the sequel), which contains a cellar.

After the initial burst of excitement ("Wow, we've got an underground passage to explore - what a place for hide n' seek!"), no-one really ever went down there. Apart from me, that is. I love it. One Sunday evening, I took a small chair and a candle down there and prayed for twenty minutes.

To me, it's a potential underground spiritual goldmine of solace. I wonder, if the Lord himself lived here, whether he'd venture down there as well. I'd love to know the mind of Christ. From what I've gleaned, Jesus would do anything to find intimacy with His Father. Even the finest vintage wines are no match for a cup of living water.

The common

"Paul, I'm getting rather concerned. Don't you want to be with your wife? Why are you trying to escape to all these places?" This may well be what you're thinking! Well, of course I do spend all the time I can with Julie but it is also essential to find space to be alone with God - preferably outdoors – but so far I have only described indoor space.

The truth is, short of a patchwork of fields beyond the boundary of the garden, the common is the next-best thing. Skipping back to chapter nine, I suggested that the local park is a great starting place for walking with God. Whether it's at sunrise or sunset, it is a 'back garden of familiarity' where a map, compass and rucksack are not required.

Its great advantage (other than the exercise you gain from doing ten laps) is that you are once again away from distractions. All that strives to compete with your quality time with the Lord is left back at the house.

And finally ...

This is where our reflections end but the adventure is only beginning! As the sun sets on this first book, I return to my question for this chapter, "Can you cut it?"

Can I? The honest truth is, not all the time. Like anyone else's family, we're not perfect by any stretch of the imagination and I do get it wrong sometimes. I'm the first to admit that but thank God for Jesus, because without him I'd be lost.

I'd be forever doing everything in my own strength and fooling myself into thinking that I'm the self-made man. The lyric at the start of this chapter sums it up perfectly: "This is the face of letting go."

We can begin to let go of our firm grip on everything and give God control in our life. Let go and let God direct us and fill us. The truth is, you don't need all these rooms and environments in which to enjoy a relationship with the Lord - these are just suggestions - but what you do need is a well. Wherever you're well is – whether it's in a field, a desert, a toilet or a stockroom – it's that quiet place in which you can be with God.

Just the two of you.

Let's have a drink ...